DON'T GET MAD,
GET RICH

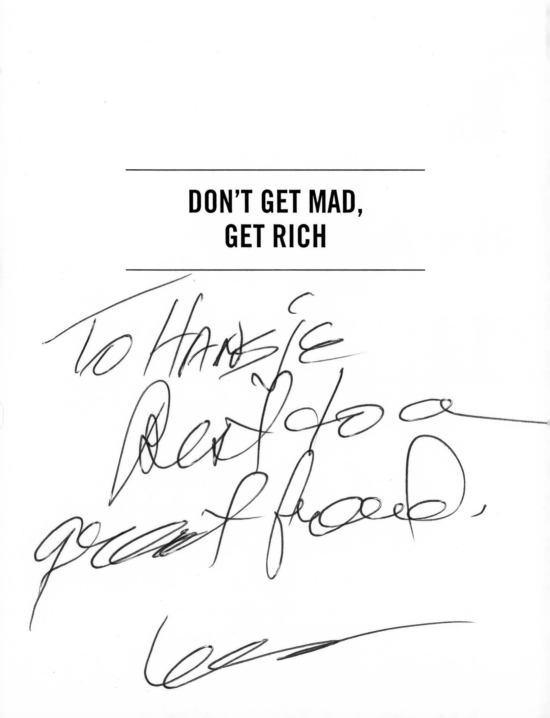

DON'T GET MAD, GET RICH

Become Financially Independent

Winston E. Allen, PhD

iUniverse, Inc.

New York Bloomington Shanghai

DON'T GET MAD, GET RICH
Become Financially Independent

Copyright © 2008 by Winston E. Allen

iUniverse books may be ordered through booksellers or by contacting:

iUniverse
1663 Liberty Drive
Bloomington, IN 47403
www.iuniverse.com
1-800-Authors (1-800-288-4677)

Because of the dynamic nature of the Internet, any Web addresses or links contained in this book may have changed since publication and may no longer be valid.

The views expressed in this work are solely those of the author and do not necessarily reflect the views of the publisher, and the publisher hereby disclaims any responsibility for them.

ISBN: 978-0-595-43250-9 (pbk)
ISBN: 978-0-595-68258-4 (cloth)
ISBN: 978-0-595-87591-7 (ebk)

Printed in the United States of America

To my parents,

Erlese and Eric Allen, who provided the

foundation that enabled me

to realize my potential and to shape the person who

I have become.

Contents

Acknowledgments

First and foremost, a special thanks to my wife, Ruby Allen. In her, I have a rare combination of a loving mate who always puts my best interests first, and who supports me at every turn. I am eternally grateful for all of the inspiration and the blessings she has brought into the writing of this work and our life together. Thanks to my son, Vaughn Allen, PhD, who provided thoughtful suggestions for this book.

Preface

Don't Get Mad, Get Rich: Become Financially Independent has its roots in my talks as a National Association of Securities Dealers (NASD) broker-dealer, financial advisor, and financial planner. During these talks, my audiences opened up about major financial issues confronting them, their families, and their college kids. Though those present had varying job experiences and educational backgrounds, most of them reported that their college age kids want a well paying job and they want to be rich.

When these college students hit their thirties and forties, many are going to be very disappointed to find that they are facing the financial and emotional trauma of unemployment due to globalization, outsourcing and offshoring—instead of becoming rich. The threat of being laid off could be lessened if they identify the jobs that are easily offshorable, and those that are not. I wrote this book in response to questions about those issues and many others. I chose the title carefully so that you would know exactly what you're getting.

I want to show you how to anticipate and navigate the often harsh realities of being an employee and having to rely on a single source of income. This book will help you cope with the probability that the job you have today will not be there tomorrow. This spiraling offshoring trend will pose major problems for millions of American workers in the coming decades who are likely to lose their jobs, and even their pensions and health insurance. It is not just low-skill service jobs like key punching and telemarketing that are offshorable, but also high-end professions like engineering and architecture. Offshoring may become the biggest political issue in economics in generations. The working public deserves an end to the nagging feelings of defeat. This book shows readers how to take charge of their lives by focusing on being financially independent instead of being mad and feeling defeated.

Why do I say to get rich instead of getting mad? Because being mad doesn't solve problems. This book demonstrates to you that you must first understand the problem. You need to analyze why you are not satisfied in your attempts to overcome financial difficulties and find the formula you need to follow to achieve your goal. I detail the steps for this process in this book.

Despairing and getting angry uses up vital energy and closes off creative juices. Such effort is better channeled into setting the goals of getting rich, having security and satisfaction with your life, and having the ability to reach out, do more, and try more. In this book, I spell out how earning one's wealth is an empowering endeavor and a worthy goal. Unfortunately, such an emphasis on getting rich can sometimes strike an exposed nerve about whether one is self-possessed and focusing too much on money. In this book, I pursue the values that come from being financially independent, such as being able to do what you're passionate about, fulfilling your dreams, and enabling you to achieve what you want out of life.

My lessons show that it is much more likely that you will be successful by moving forward with a plan and by reviewing and updating that plan than by leaving the most important aspects of your life and career to chance.

This book will help readers get on the road to financial independence by developing a wealth-building mentality. Such a mentality is built upon a foundation of planning, risk taking, and emulating successful people. I offer a peek into some real-life experiences to show how this works in practical, day-to-day life. I present steps that can lead those just starting out, as well as those looking for a career change, into their own fulfilling life experiences. I also show how planned change is important, how it worked for me, and how it can work for you.

I started as an employee, became an entrepreneur, and held a management position at a Fortune 50 corporation—all while continuing to be an entrepreneur and an inventor. Along the way, I also taught graduate-level courses at three universities and served in a top position in an international not-for-profit organization. I tell my story because I have been fortunate to have had unusual opportunities in a variety of different careers. I believe my story provides a great deal of evidence that anyone can become financially independent by following the steps I've followed.

In the three and a half years from 1968 to 1972, I went from being a high school teacher to being vigorously recruited by a Fortune 50 corporation for a fast-track position while continuing to build my company. The roots of the rest of my career can be traced to those three and a half challenging transitional years and their successful aftermath.

This book is about thriving in America and about my adventures starting with no money and entering into the worlds of finance, academia, corporate America, volunteering, and inventing. I succeeded in spite of innumerable obstacles. If I could do it, you can do it too.

Introduction

Job security in America began to wane during the 1980s and '90s. At that time, American corporations concluded that the rapid globalization of the marketplace meant they needed to compete with companies in foreign countries that had low wages, no benefits, and no unions.

Since 1995, America's largest corporations have laid off well over 10 million employees and 20 million American jobs could be lost in the coming decades. Corporate restructuring and massive job separations will continue to negatively impact the American workforce.

People who thought they would never face unemployment because they had skills in their chosen fields, worked hard, remained dedicated to their employers, and were valued by their bosses have found themselves out of work due to various factors, including: downsizing, offshoring, and corporate bankruptcy. These employees believed they could control whether they would face job separation. They were wrong. Even those who were spared unemployment found themselves constantly fearful of the possibility.

This trend has continued into the twenty-first century. Many more employees across America are likely to be separated from their jobs due to spiraling outsourcing, offshoring and downsizing. Job security is a thing of the past and people are going to have to get use to the idea of involuntary separation—sometimes four, five, or six times during their working years. Today's employee can no longer depend on a lifelong career at one company or even in one profession. In addition, the rash of corporate bankruptcies threatens the idea of a guaranteed retirement income as they eliminate employee pensions.

Because job security is a thing of the past, alternate career planning is a necessity in the face of steadily increasing offshoring and resulting job separations. In today's environment of company restructuring and reengineering, American workers need to avoid being caught with a pink slip in one hand and directions to the unemployment office in the other. This book provides solutions to this current economic situation.

Being financially independent means you are able to weather downturns in the economy and the harsh effects of downsizing that impact millions of Americans today. With financial independence, you are less dependent upon other people's whims or, most importantly, the whims of your employer. The application of my strategies is not time specific and fills a conspicuous void during times of financial reversals.

Most published books and articles dealing with layoffs limit their focus to outplacement, upgrading skills, and networking. Such aids are usually offered at a time when the jobless person is least able to benefit from them—immediately after receiving the separation notice. This upbeat and inspirational book shows you how to fortify yourself while working for others and moves you from financial dependence to financial independence, wealth, and a rich life. Being financially independent allows you to participate in activities that you find fulfilling. This book does not offer a cookbook recipe of do's and don'ts; rather, it teaches with vivid examples from real-life situations. *Don't Get Mad, Get Rich* offers a self-directed approach to prepare you *before* a layoff notice arrives. You will find in each chapter:

- Chapter Content Rationale

- Experiences to Learn From

- Tips

- Summing Up

- Your Turn for Questions

Even if you are satisfied with your current position, you may need to consider compatible ventures to ensure economic security and your ability to become financially independent. Developing and opening new avenues while employed can be critical to your economic health and solvency.

1

Create a vision, Set Goals, and Develop Plans

If you cannot think about the future, you cannot have one.
John Galsworthy (1867–1933),
Winner of the Nobel Prize for Literature

A vision serves a definite purpose. It is a perfected view of the future that determines the ideal to which you strive. If you are a painter, you imagine your paintings hanging in a famous gallery. If you are a writer, you imagine yourself being acclaimed for your great novel. Anything short of having a vision will leave you uncertain and confused as to what you want to become. What is important is that the big picture remains in your mind.

A vision of a rich life is by no means simply acquisition and ownership of resources and property. It can be far more than that, and financial independence allows you to reclaim your time. Being rich allows you to pursue interests and passions beyond day-to-day survival. It also allows you to determine for yourself how to best spend your time, opening the door for creativity, philanthropy, and other more fulfilling endeavors. Having a rich life means empowering yourself with the ability to fulfill your dreams, goals, and aspirations. Your vision should include becoming self-fulfilled and able to do what you're passionate about, expressing your creative energies, and getting what you really want out of life.

A goal is a very specific experience or event that has a definite completion date, so be sure to keep your goals *SMART*—*S*pecific, *M*easurable, *A*ttainable, *R*ealistic, *T*angible, and most important, be sure they are *your* goals. In order to crystallize your goals, develop a written plan for achieving them.

Success means achieving your planned goals. The key word is *planned.* Goals are much more likely to be valued and accomplished when they are planned. Successful people regularly set goals early, regardless of whether they are short-term or long-term, and they reassess them often. Having specific and measurable goals toward which to work and having your goals set in writing, whether they are wealth related goals or project goals, is the groundwork for success because it will keep you focused. Of course, not everything in life is planned.

The world has a curious way of parceling out surprises, both pleasant and painful. With a set of written goals firmly planted in your mind, you have a way to measure where you are compared to where you want to be. Once you adopt written goals as an essential component of your financial-independence plan, your wealth-building program moves into high gear. Some of your goals may be complex, and each might have many sub-steps that are necessary in order to accomplish the given goal. If you want to be certified as a real estate salesperson in your state within a six month period, you must complete several sub-steps including taking required courses, studying the material, and taking the exam to get licensed.

A good plan is a road map that utilizes your strengths and minimizes your weaknesses. With a realistic plan, you have both a blueprint for success and a measure against which to mark your progress. A good plan also helps you to avoid foreseeable pitfalls when possible and suggests how to best deal with them when they can't be worked around.

Will every plan work out the way you expect? No. But even when it doesn't, you have more control over your future. You can use your plan to make adjustments by matching the skills and abilities you already possess to the academic, technical, and physical requirements of your goals. You have a decided advantage over others because most people do not have any written plans. Many people who go through life without a plan end up with regrets, either for things done without thought or for things not done.

While there are many different types of plans, the following three are quite useful because they illustrate different methods you can use to enhance the skills you already possess.

A *developmental plan* is used to discover and correct deficiencies in your job skills. This plan may include participating in professional seminars, skills training, college courses, or apprenticeships. Knowing the specific academic and technical skills you need for your next endeavor is essential. If you don't possess or acquire the necessary skills, your chances of success are slim.

An *employee-employer developmental plan* helps employees and their supervisors deal with changes in the workplace proactively. It assesses an employee's skills and expertise and identifies future job requirements and needed training or other developmental experiences. This cooperative, deliberate planning process between employee and supervisor provides an opportunity to develop a strategy for achieving both personal and organizational goals.

A *business model* is one of the least understood plan types. However, since successful businesses use this type of plan when they have a new campaign, you can apply their methods by using a business model that takes you from where you are to where you want to be when you are launching your career change. Your model is solely about you; it tells you whether you are on the right track or if you need to switch gears. Adopting a business model for your personal career modeling means assessing your life experiences, especially your successes, whether they are in your education, your creative endeavors, or your other interests. Your personal model needs to reflect new technologies, new economic political climate and the worldwide competition you may face due to *offshoring* (substituting foreign for domestic labor) of white-collar jobs that were previously insulated from competition. Consider what education and training you will need to acquire to prepare you for the jobs you will want to include on your career planning short list that are least likely to be offshorable. With your personal model, you will be able to highlight the talents you have that can be molded into a better job or a business opportunity and know how you can sell yourself in either case.

Creating a vision, setting goals, and developing a plan will keep you focused on achieving your life's goals and bring you closer to the success you envision. Structuring and revising your vision as you gain experience will help you define your goals and, through planning, keep you on the right track as the inevitable twists and turns of life affect you.

Experiences to Learn From

Creating a vision, setting goals, and developing career and life plans kept me focused and put me on the path to achieving my goals. After completing my first year at New York University law school, I decided to take a leave of absence and focus on what I really wanted to do and how I planned to do it. I realized that, as great a field as law is, it would be limiting for me given the many diverse areas I wanted to explore in choosing my life's work. What I came up with was a plan to move in a new direction. I set a goal of overseas travel, postgraduate work, and starting my own business within the next five years. It was 1956, and my plan to finance this was to be a substitute teacher in the New York City public school system for a few years.

In 1961, I applied for and won a Fulbright scholarship. I found myself one of twenty American Fulbrighters studying at the Sorbonne within the historical University of Paris. If I hadn't set a specific goal of travel and higher education, I doubt that I would have searched out and found this scholarship program while I worked as a teacher. The Fulbright program turned out to be the perfect way for me to realize both travel and postgraduate education packaged neatly together. In one memorable period, my vision, goal, and plan had taken me beyond my expectations. It was while I was abroad, removed from the day-to-day activities that so often eclipse what we really want to do, that I got to see the bigger picture. While I had not yet settled on a career choice, I was able to expand my vision to embrace financial independence. In the interim, I would be able to continue to teach, find time for travel, and become self-employed.

I started in business as a sole proprietor in 1962, expanded to a corporation, Creative Investor Services, Inc. in 1966, and got a big boost with a feature article in the *New York Times* financial section in July 1968. The article caught the attention of senior management at Xerox Corporation, leading to my being vigorously recruited for a top management position in the company in January 1972. I had one overriding condition, to which

Xerox complied—the continuation of my company, Creative Investor Services, while employed at Xerox.

Tips

Tip 1. *Always have a clearly written vision for your future.*
Having a vision enhances your ability to reap the benefits that you want in life when the opportunities present themselves. Based on a vision for my future, I launched my first business.

Tip 2. *Wealth builders define a vision, establish their goals, develop a road map, and work their plan on their way to success.*
Know that you are working toward the goals in your plan, and revise your plan accordingly. I set a goal of travel and higher education that resulted in a Fulbright scholarship and study abroad.

Tip 3. *Successful leaders have written plans.*
Have a written plan on hand as you manage your future careers. My written plan made me aware that I was on the right track for a corporate executive position.

Summing Up

- A vision of a rich life is by no means simply the acquisition and ownership of resources and property. Being rich means having the ability to fulfill your goals. To have a rich life means to be truly self-fulfilled and able to do what you're passionate about, express your creative energies, and get what you really want out of life.

- Success is achieving your planned goals. Goals are much more likely to be accomplished and valued when they are written. Successful people regularly set their goals early and reassess them often.

- A plan is a road map that steers you toward your greatest strengths and toward achieving your written goals. With a realistic plan about how to reach your goals, you have both a blueprint for success and a measure against which to mark your progress.

- Wealth builders seek to discover their deficiencies and resolve to correct them using a developmental plan that may include professional seminars, college courses, skill training, or apprenticeship training. They identify job or business-relevant academic and technical skills through an assessment of their formal, informal, workplace, and volunteer training and experiences.

- Creating a vision enhances your ability to reap the benefits that you want in your life when the opportunities present themselves.

Your Turn for Questions

Take as much time as necessary to answer these and other questions at the end of each chapter. Record your answers so that you may review and adjust them at a later date. If you commit some time up front to answering these questions, you might be surprised at how realized your plans already are.

- What do you want for yourself?

- What did you love to do as a child?

- What activity do you do so intently that you don't notice time passing?

- How have your accomplishments so far helped you?

- What are your transferable skills?

- What do you feel passionate about?

- What do you value the most?

- What are your strengths?

- What changes are occurring or could occur in your place of employment?

- How will your unit or department be affected?

- How will your current job be affected?

- What new tasks or duties will you have?

- What new skills or expertise will you need?

- What current skills or expertise will you no longer be called upon to use?

- Will your job be eliminated?

- What new opportunities will be available across the workplace?

- How can you best prepare to take advantage of these opportunities?

- Is this a good time to rethink your career and plan some changes yourself?

- What kind of education (and how much) will you need to make a change?

2

Handle Multiple Careers

As life expectancy increase and the cost of living increase and retirement benefits decrease, employees find themselves working beyond retirement age and in very different careers from which they started. Some view this as an opportunity to expand meaning and purpose into later life, while others see this trend as an unfortunate economic and social reality. Today, many employees outlive the companies they work for.

The word *career* is taking on a whole new meaning as a new generation of employees move in and out of multiple jobs during their working years. This new workforce realizes that having multiple careers during the productive years of their life places them in a position of choice rather than at the mercy of the marketplace. The average worker can expect to have at least three or more careers with up to six different positions within each of those.

Consider choosing a new career as an opportunity to bring a fresh outlook and revitalization to your life, as new experiences stimulate your thought processes. The most important part of selecting a new career is also the most obvious, deciding on what you want to do. Often, this is a natural offshoot of a previous occupation. Reinventing yourself involves merging your old talents with your new skill set.

By evaluating your skills, strengths, interests, and desires (SSID), you will be able to see the relationship between what you excel at and what you value. These are the building blocks that you can use to create a new career. You can start by improving the skills you already have. Evaluating your SSID will help you decide if you need to reengineer yourself in order to be equipped for a job that isn't likely to be migrated overseas. Countries trade with one another for the same reasons that individuals, businesses and regions do: to exploit their competitive advantages. Should you choose to return to college to acquire new learning it is much easier once you understand the competitiveness and challenges that offshoring brings. One way to help you keep your job skills current during your productive work years should you become separated from a long held job due to off-shoring is to have multiple careers when possible. This will also allow you a choice as to which career you want to concentrate on in later years.

Having multiple careers is also a way to build wealth. Working the equivalent of two full-time jobs, however, can be a physical and emotional sacrifice. You need to know your capacity for a schedule that includes very long hours if you are seriously considering having multiple careers. There are those who continue simultaneous careers indefinitely and those who go full-time into their own venture while continuing on a job until the venture is successful.

When there are two equally desirable paths, there may be a way to take both at the same time. Why choose between two good options if you don't have to? It doesn't mean that everything you want to do will be equally successful, but you may just find that you have developed many useful skills and talents along the way. Even those who feel that they have a secure job should still be open to new possibilities in their careers.

There is often a conflict between a desire for financial security through salaried employment and a desire for self-employment with its greater risks. Deciding which is more important to you can be difficult, but you *can* do both.

Working for someone else, whether salaried or for an hourly wage, may make your future seem fenced in. You trade away part of your independence for cash. Your work is not at your will, but mandated by management. Your time is not under your own control. You are trapped by your need for regular income and tied to the obligations of your job. Other than annual salary increases, quickly consumed by the rising cost of living and taxes, you have limited ways of gaining extra income, unless you are willing and able to take a second job or start your own business on the side.

It is important to note, however, that there are very real advantages to having a regular income while you are building your independent venture. A job presents you with specific income on a regular basis. A great asset is that you have time beyond the workday that is yours to use at your discretion.

One option is to take your salary from your current job and put it to work while you also work for yourself. E-commerce—online enterprises—is a way for small start-up businesses to get off the ground. You can then have the security of a steady income to finance your online business until it is profitable and you are able to explore other alternatives.

Business owners do not have to follow orders or observe working hours set by someone else. It provides them with the rare opportunity to prove to themselves and society what they can accomplish. Although being a business owner is hard work, it is often exhilarating and rewarding. In addition, many business owners create wealth by building businesses and selling them at a profit, producing fortunes for themselves.

Recently, a person reported on a visit to a spa and her enthusiasm with a weight machine. She thought how great it would be if the spa in her hometown had this type of machine for exercising. She began to think about how she could start such a business in her own community. Another person, while acquiring refinancing for her home, found out that most of the mortgage brokers worked part-time and out of their homes as independent contractors, earning additional income to supplement their current salary. The first person explored the spa idea, and the other became a mortgage broker working at home.

Once you learn the basics of one enterprise, you can transfer what you have learned into another enterprise and discover another avenue to make money. In this uncertain employment climate, easing into self-employment in this way could be a lucrative option.

Experiences to Learn From

The path leading me to multiple careers began when I took a leave of absence following that first year of law school. Needing an income while deciding what I should do, I went to the New York City Board of Education to have my name entered on a per-diem *substitute teacher* roster. I was directed to the office of the superintendent, Dr. Lillian Rashkis, who, after an interview, offered me instead the opportunity to take a teacher's examination that day that could provide me with a license to begin teaching full-time the next day. The speed of all of this made me pause. I would be committing to a full-time job, but I could use the salary. I decided to go for it. That afternoon, to my surprise, I found myself with a teaching license for the 600 school system and an assignment to report the next morning to PS 611 at 138th Street and Paul Avenue, a section of the South Bronx popularly known as "Fort Apache" because of its substantial number of active street gangs. The 600 schools were schools for at-risk kids, assigned there from regular schools usually for disciplinary reasons. To ensure everyone's safety, the principal and the teachers greeted each student every morning as they entered the building with a daily frisk. There was a large container placed at the door for the contraband that we found. We usually collected a number of zip guns and knives.

According to the official Board of Education bulletin incidentally, 600 schoolteachers were licensed and specially selected for their skill in working with this type of student. The school offered English, social studies, mathematics, science, business training, woodworking, printing, and metal work. Public School 611's staff included about fifteen academic teachers, an industrial education teacher, a school secretary, and a principal. Individual counseling and guidance was available from an on-call counselor. Class size was small. Typically, we had fifteen boys assigned to each teacher, and with about 30 percent absenteeism on average, I regularly had about ten boys in my class on any given day. I was able to give students individual attention and work with them one-on-one, which was a new experience for them.

Despite having been designated as seriously emotionally disturbed young men, many of whom had "rap sheets," they were amenable once a trusting relationship was created. With the exception of their industrial arts class, all of their classes were with their assigned homeroom teacher for the entire day. This was a challenge for both the students, with their short attention span, and for their teachers, who were responsible for a restless and potentially volatile group of energetic young men.

Motivating them was the key to keeping them engaged in the classroom activities. I sought out their interests individually and discovered that many had musical interests and enjoyed performing. In addition to the prescribed three *Rs*, I decided to start a small instrumental group. I got a set of drums, and a few other instruments were donated. Our music sessions grew to include more students and more instruments, and we had regular practice sessions that livened up the school corridors. My education at the prestigious High School of Music and Art became useful in a job where I had not expected to draw on it. The principal, Mr. Jones, asked me if I would continue the group and expand it to include other kids in the school during my second year. He promoted my instrumental group as the "first school orchestra" in the 600 school system. This wouldn't be the last time my efforts beyond the norm without preplanning were recognized and rewarded. One key to being a successful wealth builder is to recognize opportunities to improve upon the norm.

During my second year, Mr. Jones called me in and recalled how I was initially only interested in a per diem substitute teaching position. He was impressed with my success with the students and with the school orchestra. He thought my talents would be wasted in my present assignment and I would soon leave teaching. He asked if I would consider staying in teaching if I could get assigned on the high school level. I would have to take the high school teaching exam, and he would recommend me to the principal of one of the top academic high schools in the city. I decided to go for it. I'd discovered that there was a lot for me to give to students and a lot for me to learn in teaching.

After the exam, I was assigned to DeWitt Clinton High School in the North Bronx teaching economics and history. Teaching at Clinton in the late 1950s and early 1960s was worlds apart from P.S. 611. It's a school that opened its doors for the first time in Manhattan in 1897. In 1929, the school moved to a 21 acre campus on Mosholu Parkway in the North Bronx, where it is presently located. It had a well trained faculty of devoted teachers. The principal, Walter Degnan, a strong leader in both academics and athletics, with winning citywide championship teams kept the school well tuned. The school had an extensive Youth and Adult Center for after-school and evening activities, where I taught piano to adults. The Dewitt Clinton Alumni Association was proud of its famous members, whose names helped attract more students from junior high schools throughout the city. Noted alums included actors, authors, luminaries, and politicians such as Avery Fisher, Lionel Trilling, William Zeckendorf, George Cukor, Vito Marcantonio, Martin Balsam, James Baldwin, Neil Simon, Gil Noble, Richard Rogers, Lorenz Hart, Charles Rangel, Bernard Kalb, William Kunstler, Paul O'Dwyer, Stanley Kramer, Countee Cullen, Daniel Schorr, Adolph Green, and Paddy Cheyefsky.

After three years at Clinton, I was ready to take a break and pursue my desire to travel and discovered that an opportunity for travel and higher education could be available through the Fulbright scholarship program. I applied for and won a Fulbright scholarship to study in Paris in 1961. I left for France and studied at the Sorbonne. Returning to the States, I resumed teaching at Clinton and soon after launched my first business as a principal of a broker-dealer firm, licensed to sell general securities for the accounts of others and for my own account.

In February of 1968, after ten years at Clinton, I submitted my resignation to Principal Degnan, informing him that I would be leaving in June to consider a position on the college level. He asked me to reconsider because "you wouldn't want to regret your move some years from now." He said, "Teachers are not known to walk away from such a great school and a coveted tenured position."

I thanked him for ten truly inspiring years at Clinton. I ended my high school teaching career in June of 1968, a tumultuous year in our nation's history with the assassinations of Martin Luther King, Jr., and Robert F. Kennedy, the height of the Viet Nam War, the violent disruption of the Democratic National Convention in Chicago, and the first major New

York City teachers' strike, pitting colleagues and friends against one another.

In preparation for a position on a college level, I needed to matriculate into a doctoral degree program, and I got admitted provisionally to Fordham University. While in the doctoral program, I accepted a job in the City University system at Queensborough Community College (QCC) as assistant professor, heading up the College Discovery Program. This position had longer hours, more challenges, and a lesser salary than DeWitt Clinton High School, but it was a college-level administrative position that I valued. My new position as director of the College Discovery Program dealt with students who had failed to achieve either acceptable high school grades or satisfactory scholarship aptitude test results for college admission, and were also economically deprived. Economic deprivation might influence college potential, but it doesn't necessarily negate it. The City University, therefore, experimented with methods by which college potential might be encouraged and measured.

My careers soon included my day job at QCC, night classes at Fordham, and my entrepreneurial venture as a broker-dealer I realized eventually that going from day job to night school while still continuing to run my company was exhausting and put me on a slow track to my doctorate. To speed up the process, I resigned from QCC at the end of my first year. I completed the course work for the Ph.D. program, which I considered my union card for college teaching, and was offered the position of instructor at Fordham while finishing my dissertation.

I once again found myself expanding my multiple careers when I proposed a special summer school overseas program for Fordham's sponsorship. Fordham was very enthusiastic about it. It would be conducted in the summer when city-wide teachers, administrators, and graduate students could attend. The program took an expectant year of planning, and its implementation date was July 1972. By that time, I had just started my job as a consultant at Xerox, and they granted me a four-week leave to conduct the program. In the summer of 1972, I took the group to London, and Durham, England, and Carmarthen, Wales for Fordham's first internship program for teachers and administrators, formally known as the International Education Institute's Workshop in Open Education.

Balancing multiple careers is not for everyone, but for those who can do it, they realize the benefits long after the grueling schedule is a thing of the past. I have often been asked how I managed multiple careers and night classes. It is easier when you know that you are working toward achieving what you set out to do.

Tips

Tip 1. *Consider multiple careers.*
Realizing your self-employment dream with a new venture, along with your regular job, and continuing your education helps put you on your path to financial independence. I operated a broker-dealer business while a college administrator.

Tip 2. *Salary should not be the sole factor to consider when making a career-change decision.*
Viewing your career from a larger perspective than salary alone can pave the way to a better opportunity with better long-term compensation and benefits. I did this when I left high school teaching for a position at QCC and later Fordham University, where I obtained a doctorate—all of which led to my being hired by Xerox Corporation. My salary and other compensation eventually far exceeded what I would have earned as a high school teacher.

Tip 3. *Wealth builders do more than one thing at a time.*
Multiple careers can be profitable. I was rarely in just one line of work or business at one time.

Summing Up

- Multiple careers can be profitable.

- Wealth builders do more than one thing at a time.

- Wealth builders realize that it is difficult to make a lot of money doing just one thing. Working two full-time ventures can be tough and a physical sacrifice. You need to know your capacity for a strenuous schedule that may include very long hours if you are seriously considering having multiple careers.

- There is a conflict between salaried employment and its greater financial security and self-employment and its greater risk. You try to decide which is more important to you. Although it is a hard decision, you can have them both. Once you learn the basics in one enterprise, you can transfer what you have learned into another pursuit and discover another avenue to make money.

- Consider multiple careers. Realizing your self-employment dream by operating a business along with your regular job helps put you on your path to financial independence.

- Salary should not be the sole factor to consider when making a career-change decision. Viewing your career from a larger perspective than salary alone can pave the way to a better opportunity with better long-term compensation and benefits.

Your Turn for Questions

- Do you have the stamina to work twelve-hour days?

- Can you maintain focus on more than one responsibility at a time?

- How might you seek out multiple sources of income?

- Are you organized with your time?

- Are you a creative thinker?

- Are you the kind of person that recognizes a need and finds solutions for meeting that need?

- What are some examples of recognizing needs and finding solutions in your own life?

3

Invest in Yourself

The people who get on in this world are the people who get up and look
for the circumstances they want; and, if they can't
find them, make them.
George Bernard Shaw (1856–1950),
dramatist

For those who want to one day run their own show, corporate America
turns out to be a pretty good training ground. Most people who think "it's
not my job" have it wrong. That attitude will make you miss out on valuable possibilities that can often lead to your next promotion or a more
lucrative venture. Whether you are aware of it or not, whatever job you're
in gives you access to critical knowledge and skills. When you move to
your next situation, you take with you what you have acquired, and that
knowledge and those skills will determine your degree of success.

A work-to-learn strategy of investing in yourself shows how you can use
the opportunities in your present job to develop the knowledge and skills
for your next situation. This strategy lets you view every assignment or job
you're in as an opportunity to learn and become the best at what you do. It
will also show you how investing in yourself calls for the initiative to anticipate problems, imagination to take action when situations arise, and ingenuity to seize opportunities. If your company provides a formal training
program for you, then you are especially fortunate. If not, you can still
acquire new knowledge, develop new skills, and find satisfaction in your
work.

Changes in the workplace are happening at an amazing pace. Additional training and education enhances an employee's value, because those
with the dedication to give up some of their discretionary time to studies

and self-education possess the qualities that make for growth and leadership. An important trait that successful people have in common is the commitment to knowledge that gives them control and authority over their destiny. Keep an eye open for opportunities to accumulate wealth by acquiring new technical information, learning, and unique knowledge essential in today's fast-moving economy.

Two kinds of learning exists that affect wealth accumulation: one is specialized learning and the other is general learning. General learning is of little use in making big money. The learning that you will benefit from most in wealth creation is acquired through specialized learning.

Successful people usually continue to develop specialized learning related to their profession or business. This is especially important in taking on a new venture. When working in a new area, the goal toward which you are working determines what particular knowledge you need to acquire. Successful people know that they must obtain accurate information from dependable sources.

Having and applying specialized learning can create an advantaged position. When skillfully directed, structured and utilized, specialized learning leads to wealth building. The development of great wealth in this information and communication age that has seen an upward march of technology in recent decades, calls for the use of specialized learning or technical learning. The opportunity to gain new technical skills has never been better. Information available on the Internet brings knowledge you seek right to your home, office, and library. As technology continues to advance, the quality of now-familiar modes of communication (Blackberries, cell phones, video conferencing, Internet) and entirely new forms of communication will be invented. One clear implication of the forward march of technology, is that a growing array of services will become deliverable electronically.

The people who make real money in America often have a basic understanding of many important sources of technical or unique learning. As the economic situation gets more complicated and the competition for the dollar gets tougher, wealth builders develop a greater appreciation for study and analysis.

Successful people in all fields know that all professions and occupations now demand more specialization. However, technical information and learning needs to be organized and used for a definite purpose, with practical written plans and the awareness that the march of technology and the widening array of services will become increasingly deliverable electronically. If your desire for change and financial success is great enough, you will take the necessary action and reap greater financial rewards.

The wealth builder does not need to know all that must be known to run a venture profitably at all times. There are experts who can be hired for specific purposes who have technical knowledge. This should give encouragement and hope to those with ambition to accumulate wealth but who do not possess the necessary education to supply such technical information or expertise as may be required.

People aspiring to be successful can help themselves by building self-esteem, because self-esteem and confidence are essential characteristics for wealth building. In fact, there is no value judgment more important in becoming financially independent than how a person judges himself. The relationship between self-esteem and productive work is evident when we examine the level of goals that people set for themselves. The higher the self-esteem a person has, the more that person seeks demanding challenges, the more desire and use that person makes of his or her capabilities to the fullest extent, and the more eager that person is for new experiences.

Perhaps, as more jobs migrate overseas and as your company looks for qualified English speaking workers who will happily work for a fractions of what you earn, you may consider additional education or retraining for those jobs that are likely to remain in the United States. You will need a combination of preparation, persistence, and hard work if you are to succeed. Seizing opportunities and investing in yourself can produce financial security.

Experiences to Learn From

Using the experiences of others and how they overcame obstacles in their early lives, I invited several professionals to be guest speakers at the College Discovery Career Opportunity Seminar that I organized at Queensborough Community College. I hoped to show students how, by emulating successful people, they could become successful in spite of their early years. Two of the professionals who shared their personal stories showed how in spite of early deficiencies in their education, they overcame seemingly insurmountable hurdles to become very successful in their careers.

A physician at Memorial Sloan Kettering Cancer Center immigrated as a young man to the United States from Trinidad without a high school diploma. He took an equivalency examination in New York and then went on to New York University, where he graduated near the top of his class. He then applied to a medical school in Heidelberg, Germany, and overcame inherent difficulties in completing his medical studies in a foreign language. He told the students that after he passed his medical board exams in the United States, he earned his license to practice his profession as a medical doctor in a leading New York City hospital.

An owner of an executive search firm who had grown up in Mississippi with almost no formal high school education came to New York City in his late teens. With remedial work in the basic courses, he was able to attend Rhodes High School, a private school in New York City, at night for several years. He graduated and took courses at City College. He later became a consultant in the field of personnel placement for General Electric, and with that experience he was able to start and operate his own executive search firm. He explained how it was possible to build a business that was successful, even with a substandard early education, with developed skills, persistence, and hard work. He also helped them become aware of a new career and they leaned about his work as a business owner. He then explained to students how an executive search firm helps corporations find top talent, which can be the difference between success and failure for a company. In the course of doing business, the search firm accepts resumes from applicants seeking executive positions. He related how he had a talent for engaging those who came to his company and that he enjoyed working with people

Building on the response to this enrichment program, I followed it with another motivational event at QCC. I invited actor, author, and civil-rights leader Ossie Davis to speak to the CD students. His talk was very inspirational, and the students raved about it. His message is just as important today as it was in the late '60s. Ossie Davis's theme was: take the hand you are dealt and learn to play it so that it gives the results that you want. His message was very inspiring to these students, many of whom felt they had been dealt a hand that was not going to get them very far. Now they talked about taking advantage of the opportunities at the college that came their way instead of feeling sorry for themselves. Many of them came to me after his talk and told me that they felt that it gave them a new reason to be hopeful and to work harder in their courses. A few said that after graduating from QCC, they were now inspired to go on to a four-year college for further education and more career options.

My maxim has been to try the difficult. The tougher the assignment, the more you learn. If you are successful, you can end up doing something meaningful and reap the benefits, as I did when recognized by those in a position to award my efforts through advancements and promotion, opening the door to my career at DeWitt Clinton High School. As I look back, voluntarily creating the school orchestra at PS 611 was the first of a number of instances when I invested in myself by using what I'd gained from solving problems I had been faced with earlier. The lessons I had learned in creating PS 611's school orchestra propelled me to create the economics club at DeWitt Clinton and later the International Education Institute's Workshop at Fordham University for overseas study in England and Wales. Again, I took advantage of an opportunity to be an added asset in my job.

Students at DeWitt Clinton were accustomed to the usual extracurricular activities such as the drama club, art clubs, foreign language clubs, and the like. But the economics club was the first of its kind. It attracted students with a common interest, and they learned more about the subject by delving deeper into it. We went on field trips to financial sites like the New York Stock Exchange. We went to corporate sites like Johnson and Johnson Corporation in Raritan, New Jersey, and A. S. Beck Shoe Company in New York, so that the students could experience behind-the-scenes operations of two different companies. The club's members appeared on a couple of radio and television programs. They talked about their activities and interest in being members of a club that focused on economics and finance, perhaps leading to careers in those fields.

My community involvements and extracurricular activities were both rewarding to me and of lasting value, because when I launched my company, I had a cadre of contacts. Some of those became clients and some remained with me for dozens of years.

I was still teaching at the time, but in operating Creative Investor Services, I wanted to be certain I was able to handle a variety of my clients' needs, so I sought ways to expand our product line to include life insurance. I needed to quickly become licensed to sell life insurance, and proceeded to take the exam.

Since I lacked life insurance sales experience, I asked to tag along with two of the most experienced salesmen from Presidential Life Insurance Company. This took a lot of my time, but I was eager to learn the insurance business. The hands-on skill and knowledge I acquired from two experienced salesmen was invaluable.

Phil Wang, one of two selected salesmen, had been selling life insurance for more than twenty years. Phil's style was formal and businesslike, taking early control of the sales presentation by peppering his customers with a series of leading questions that led them through the key features and benefits of the policy. His wrap-up was nearly always followed with a signed contract and check in hand. I was reminded that what I'd achieve in my selling career was entirely up to me.

Bob Hirsh, the second salesman, was older than Phil and had sold insurance much of his adult life. Bob's style fit his personality just as Phil's fit his. Bob was effusive and personable. I will never forget the experience of joining Bob on his sales calls. One evening, Bob said to me, "I am going to close at least a dozen policies tonight, young man. Want to come along?" A dozen sales in one evening was a sizeable goal for even the most experienced salesman, and I jumped at the chance to see how he planned to do it and what I could learn from his process.

We met at the Hudson River pier on 125th Street and boarded a chartered party boat for a cruise up the Hudson. Bob was very popular with the crowd, bestowing hugs and kisses on the women and handshakes and slaps on the backs of the men. He fit right in with the environment and the music and the beat, but that didn't affect his organization or his timing. Every document he needed was color coded and ready for the close. He knew which benefits each of his clients would hook on to, even though the benefits for each differed. By the end of the evening, Bob had surpassed his target, and although it was a bit unorthodox, his style was a lasting lesson that selling could be fun and no activity is more dependent on individual initiative than selling, as you have the freedom to become as successful as you'd like to be.

Not only had I seen two distinctly different styles in action—one was clinical and the other was very flamboyant—but I realized that they both had one thing in common. Both had specialized learning essential to their being successful salesmen. Both men had high self-esteem and were very confident in their sales ability and their people skills. They knew their product and their competition's products so thoroughly that they could anticipate and handle any questions or objections without hesitation.

Unlike selling securities, life insurance sales are different and also more difficult. Why? Because successful salesmen know that they must sell benefits. When they sell securities, cars, and home furnishings, they sell the tangible benefits to the person who will benefit personally from their purchase. When selling life insurance to a prospect, they are selling to their clients, benefits that will be realized by the beneficiary.

Professional salesmen have specialized learning, and both Phil and Bob were so equipped. They knew that giving all of their attention to the prospect was the key to their success, and they were prepared to handle various personalities, situations, and objections. For example, their presentation might be relaxed, alert, or businesslike; other times they could be pleasant, intense, candid, or personal. Their specialized knowledge didn't stop there. The phrasing of a single answer to an objection could be fast, medium, or slow. They could speak soft, moderate, or loud. They could be respectful, friendly, or aggressive. When they applied variations to aspects of their selling sequence, they had a huge inventory for their responses, and finding the perfect fit for every prospect became easy for them. If there is any way the sale could be made, they were able to make it.

Tips

Tip 1. *Taking extra initiative in your job often leads to positive developments.*
Showing initiative can lead to being spotlighted, with possible opportunities opening up for you. I drew on the lessons I learned in creating the economics club at DeWitt Clinton High School.

Tip 2. *Emulate people who demonstrate the ability to accomplish uncommon things professionally or in business.*
Researching the biographies of successful people who overcame difficulties in early life can enrich you and help you in overcoming your deficiencies. By introducing examples of successful professionals who had early educational difficulties to my students, I offered them the hope that they could overcome their challenges and accomplish great things.

Tip 3. *Upgrade your knowledge base continually.*
By continuing to obtain knowledge and acquire new skills, you increase your effectiveness as you market and sell your products or services. I studied product benefits and features so I could more suitably—and profitably—match them with my prospective clients' needs. I also studied sales techniques and observed experienced salesmen at their craft.

Tip 4. *Consider compatible business opportunities that can uniquely fit into your present company.*
By adding another set of business opportunities, you can increase your profit base. Adding a life insurance component to my product line was a natural fit that offered my customers additional benefits.

Summing Up

- A work-to-learn strategy of investing in yourself lets you view every assignment or job as an opportunity to learn and become the best at what you can do.

- Investing in yourself calls for the initiative to anticipate problems, imagination to take action when situations arise, and ingenuity to seize opportunities.

- Preparation, persistence, and hard work can remove many obstacles from your path and help you gain friendly interest and support from those who have the power to put you on the path of opportunity.

- An important trait that successful people have in common is the commitment to knowledge that gives them control and authority over their destiny. The people who make real money in America often have a basic understanding of many important sources of information. As the economic situation gets more complicated and the competition for the dollar gets tougher, wealth builders develop a greater appreciation for study and analysis.

- Successful people never stop acquiring technical or unique learning related to their profession or business. This is especially important when taking on a new venture. When working in a new area, they try to determine what specialized or unique learning they need to acquire and try to ensure that they have accurate information from dependable sources.

- Acquiring technical expertise can be used to build an advantaged position, especially if it is unique knowledge. You may create a monopoly position for yourself, which can lead to wealth building. The accumulation of great fortunes has occurred through unique knowledge.

- The relationship between self-esteem and productive work is evident when you examine the level of goals people set for themselves. The higher the self-esteem of people, the more demanding the challenges they will seek, the more eager they will be for new challenges, and the greater the use they will make of their capabilities.

- Researching the biographies of successful people who overcame difficulties in early life can enrich you and help you in overcoming your deficiencies.

- By continuing to acquire new skills and expertise, you increase your effectiveness as you market and sell yourself and your products or services.

Your Turn for Questions

- How would you go about determining your academic and technical deficiencies?

- How can you address these deficiencies and invest in yourself?

- How might you alter your behavior to increase your wealth?

- What technical information do you believe you need to acquire in order to gain financial independence?

- What ways can you go about gaining that knowledge?

- What might you be willing to do to gain unique learning?

4

Find Your Niche

There are two great days in a person's life—the day we are born
and the day we discover why.
William Barclay (1907–1978),
theologian

A niche is a place, employment, or activity for which you are best suited.
You may fit into more than one niche. If you find that the niche you are in
is not right for you, change the trend in which your life is going; the trend
will continue until you change it. Change your approach. Seek out information that can help you. Once you are comfortable with your niche, you
can start living for that purpose.

Take a global view of your world and where you fit in. Sometimes the
answers are not in your "backyard." Expand your view through travel,
joining organizations, and taking courses. For some people, running and
managing their own venture such as a business or investment is their
niche. For others, public service is their niche. Devoting your life to something you are passionate about and discovering your purpose in life can be
an incredible experience. People experience fulfillment through volunteer-
ism, and the personal identification that comes from an association with
worthy organizations.

Wealth builders tend to be self-made people, and most find their niche
in making money. Having found their niche, they exhibit a positive attitude toward learning what they need to know about the things that are
important in acquiring wealth and knowledge.

To find your niche, choose interests and talents that are tops on your
list of what you would like to do in life. Also, what are the activities that
you do well that serve a need. If you have special talents or skills that you

wish to make your life's work, see if they will fit with the needs of others; this is especially true for those considering starting a business based on a special talent they have. If you are proficient in numbers, consider book-keeping and accounting as a small at-home business; if you are a people-centered person, sales may be your niche, and if your last job was as a researcher, consider proofreading or freelance writing.

Experiences to Learn From

Seeking my niche contributed to my winning a Fulbright scholarship to the University of Paris. My goals of travel and education were being achieved, and I was feeling very positive about my future. I returned home after the Fulbright ended and resumed teaching at DeWitt Clinton High School. At about this time, I launched my first business, a National Associ-ation of Securities Dealers (NASD) broker-dealer firm. I had yet to decide whether I was lining up a new venture that would replace my teaching job or planning to work them both together. Although I had my eye on a col-lege teaching position, I was not yet ready to leave Clinton, as it was a great place to work, and my teaching schedule allowed me enough time to keep my company growing. I continued at Clinton for the next six years but tried a few additional things as I sought my niche.

The Fulbright was a great way to see the bigger picture. On our trip over to Europe, the original plan was for the twenty Fulbrighters to sail on the SS *United States* to France. The SS *United States* was then the fastest liner on the seas, but the trip still would take about a week. It was a long-standing tradition that the Fulbrighters would sail together so that they could get acquainted. The ship's leisurely pace and group dining would give us a chance to get to know each other, to meet other passengers, and to just enjoy the trip. Plans were in place for Madam Colette Stourdse, professor at the University of Paris, to conduct the shipboard orientation on behalf of the United States Educational Commission for France.

However, plans changed at the last minute when a maritime strike tied up all ships. The Fulbright Committee had to resort to their backup plan, and so all twenty of us, ten men and ten women, boarded a Pan Am plane at JFK Airport and flew directly to Paris. There, we were met by Madam

Domique, who was our host and guide throughout our Fulbright experience. We were herded onto a bus for the ride to the University of Paris area. The bus let us off at a quaint hotel on the left bank, where we would be housed and given rooms near the Sorbonne on the rue des écoles. We all were in high spirits and delighted to be one of the chosen twenty Fulbright scholars. There was no need for an attitude adjustment with our group. We felt like winners, and our attitudes showed it.

The next morning, I was raring to go in a new city that was unfolding around me. Madame Domique, who was meticulous about every detail, met us for a briefing before we traveled to the Sorbonne and started classes. I began to keep a diary in a leather-bound book because there was so much I wanted to remember. As Fulbright students, we were officially referred to as grantees, and we were experiencing a warm welcome in our new environment.

The Fulbright program was divided into three phases. The first phase was devoted to the academic program that included morning lectures and afternoon discussions in economics and history with grantees required to attend all sessions. Classes were held at the Institutes d'Etudes or (Institutes of Political Studies), which is a part of the University of Paris. Four distinguished French university professors shared the responsibility of conducting the lectures including professors Jean-Baptiste Duroselle, University of Notre-Dame; Maurice Levy-Leboyer, Paris Institute of Political Studies; and Raymond Polin, University of Lille, France. The lectures were supplemented with discussion sessions.

The second phase consisted of organized visits to points of historical significance in and around France. Our travel included trips through Normandy, Brittany, and the Loire Valley. Grantees traveled by chartered bus throughout France. We were accompanied by Madam Domique, a professional French guide and an American staff member of the U.S. Educational Commission for France. The most memorable stop for me was the landing beaches of Omaha and Arromanches, the entrenchments on the cliffs looking down on the beaches that seemed impenetrable, and the seemingly endless grave markings of American soldiers.

The third phase provided time for personal travel by the grantees at our discretion. During weekends, holidays, and class breaks, I traveled with my thirty-dollars-per-month Eurail Pass on the great European Express trains throughout Europe and into North Africa without even having to stop to make a reservation. I couldn't wait for Friday afternoons when, right after the final discussion session class for the week, I would be packed and heading for the Gard de Nord railroad station, ready to board the next express train to a new city and country. Where I would go depended on the posted schedule for the overnight express trains. The overnight train had another bonus of eliminating the cost of a hotel while I had the excitement of awakening in a new country at dawn the next day.

It was 1961, and I could find myself in Barcelona, Rome, Munich, Geneva, Copenhagen, Amsterdam, or Vienna. On extended trips I went as far north in Europe as Stockholm, Sweden and Oslo, Norway and as far south through Spain across the Straits of Gibraltar, into North Africa, where I ventured further south to exotic Marrakech in Morocco. Marrakech took me back centuries into another exquisite world of camels, snake charmers, and souks (outdoor markets), packed with all kinds of goods. On another trip to Spain, I visited the cities of Granada, Cordoba, and Seville, with their Moorish architecture; and on a future trip I visited Israel, Turkey, and Greece.

One European city, Copenhagen, had a unique program that introduced visitors to Danish families who signed up to host visitors to their city in their home. The program was promoted as "Meet the Danes." Arriving in Copenhagen by train, I was directed to phone "Meet the Danes" to obtain a host family's contact number for a weekend visit, and upon getting directions, I hopped in a taxi and was greeted at their home when I arrived. My Danish hosts spoke English, and it was truly a great way to meet people you would not otherwise meet, learn a bit about their city, gain an understanding of their way of life, and share experiences. Being an African American only sparked their interest and our discussions.

They were especially interested in the unlikely aspect of hosting a visitor raised in Harlem. I always felt fortunate to live in a bustling, metropolitan neighborhood, only a few blocks from a large lake in Central Park with all of its recreational possibilities. I answered their questions about my parents: my mother came to the United States from Grenada as a young woman and my father from Jamaica, both via Ellis Island.

To me, the Harlem I lived in at that time was just plain old Harlem, a bunch of varied neighborhoods where some residents were well off, some fallen on hard times, and where most people tried their best to make a decent living and raise a family. Many of the residents like my family were focused on education, self-improvement, community uplifting, and in maintaining a positive attitude about life.

Harlem was the home to many black professionals: artists, musicians, and writers some of whom I knew personally like Dr. John Henrik Clarke, a well-known historian who shared his passion of African-American history and the Harlem Renaissance with me. I filled in my Danish hosts with some other important aspects of the Harlem community, particularly the Schomburg Library, a center for culture and research and one of the world's richest sources for learning about black history. I had always had a fascination with history and spent many hours poring over original documents of historical figures like Frederick Douglas and W.E.B. DuBois and books about the arts, science, education and politics. I was energized seeing all that had been accomplished before me—and was inspired to try to do something meaningful with my life.

I returned home from Paris, and continued my teaching career until I resigned in 1968, seven years later. Three years after that seminal year of 1968, I began a ten-year stint at Xerox Corporation. Service to the community became an expanding part of my corporate life. Those of us in upper management at Xerox were encouraged by CEO, Peter McColough, to seek out experiences in the larger community like university teaching, public speaking and membership on boards.

I became an adjunct professor of management sciences at George Washington University and American University graduate business schools for several semesters and accepted speaking engagements at community and business organizations. I was appointed as a corporate member of the United States Committee for UNICEF and served for eight years. I learned a great deal about the importance of focusing on the needs of the world's children during my tenure from luminaries such as chairman Hugh Downes, along with other corporate members including Norman Cousins, Mrs. Arthur Anderson, Mrs. Chester Bowles, Mrs. Hodding Carter, and Dr. Frederick H. Lovejoy, Jr.

The UNICEF experience brought home to me how "soul satisfying" working for the welfare of children throughout the world could be. The UNICEF Board relied very heavily on volunteers, starting with children who used their trick-or-treat UNICEF orange boxes to fundraise impressive amounts. The receipts from one single Halloween night totaled in excess of $3.5 million for UNICEF, which was augmented by revenues from UNICEF greeting-card sales that topped $6 million in one year.

Along the way, in 1975, I served as the liaison member to the board of the National Advisory Council on Minorities in Engineering (NACME), a national organization designed to bring about a tenfold increase in the number of minority engineering graduates within the next decade.

In late 1975, my new responsibilities at Xerox brought me to corporate headquarters in Stamford, Connecticut. I moved with my family to Westport, Connecticut, and continuing the Xerox philosophy of giving back to the community I joined the Xerox Speakers Forum. I spoke at several community-service organizations, including the Lyons Club in New Canaan and the Discussion Information Group of Single Adults (DIGOSA) Club in Norwalk, Connecticut.

Soon after I moved to Westport, I was appointed to the Westport Conservation Commission and served as chairman for four years. I chaired the public hearings and we dealt with wetlands, open space and site permits. After twelve years with the commission, I was appointed alternate member of Westport's zoning board of appeals, serving an additional twelve years.

During the same period, I was invited to join Rotary, the world's largest international service organization with a global network of 1.2 million volunteers worldwide, and after eight years I was selected to be district governor. Following my term as governor, I was elected chairman of the governing board for the training of all incoming Rotary Club presidents in seven districts throughout New England and Canada.

My wife, Ruby, and I traveled widely throughout the Far East (including China, Thailand, Malaysia, and Indonesia), Australia, New Zealand, and Central and South America (including Guatemala, Mexico, Chile, Peru, Equador, Argentina, and Brazil). As Rotary district governor, our travels continued. In 1999, we served as volunteers with a Rotary dental team in villages in Jeremie, Haiti, to provide free dental services to families, many with severe dental problems. While in Jeremie we celebrated the villagers' achievement in building what Rotary called "happy houses," the cement houses that replaced thatched-roof huts. The happy houses were built by the villagers using contributions from Rotary district 7980 in Connecticut.

We made another memorable trip to South Africa in 2001 during my year as district governor. We were among six Rotarian couples, selected to join a Rotary vice president and his wife, on a three-week visit to inspect Rotary Foundation projects throughout South Africa. Some of the projects that we visited were the Hospice for AIDS Orphans near Johannesburg, a St. John's Mobile Eye Clinic providing eye exams and glasses for the village, and a project that provided donated books for the South African schools. In one case, a truckload of twenty-seven thousand books was donated. We also visited in Cape Town, the only children's hospital in sub-Saharan Africa, a center for deaf children, and a cerebral palsy and rehabilitation clinic in Randburg. We visited many schools where children were learning in spite of the absence of books and other school materials. Kids were eager to learn, and many of the elementary school children had to start their six-mile walk to school each day before dawn in order to arrive on time.

All Rotary trips were at our own expense, as 100 percent of the approximately $70 million raised annually by the Rotary Foundation are used solely for humanitarian projects, and in addition to all of our many other charitable giving, we also became Rotary Foundation major donors.

After my year as district governor, I organized my own 501(c)(3) foundation to establish scholarships for entrepreneurs and college students.

Tips

Tip 1. *Enhance your credentials.*
Enhancing your credentials enables you to increase your career options and marketability and broadens your horizons. Receiving a Fulbright scholarship to study at the University of Paris enhanced my credentials.

Tip 2. *View volunteer work as a knowledge and skill builder.*
Contributing your services as a volunteer builds self-esteem and enhances your knowledge and skill. My volunteer work helped me to develop an understanding of many new areas.

Summing Up

- Finding the right niche is a must on your way to financial independence. Of all the things that determine your success or failure in life, seeking and finding your niche is one of the most important.

- At times, your attitude and confidence will determine if you are in the right niche. When in doubt, you will need to convince yourself that the future process is worthy of your effort, and will enable you to become prone to success rather than failure. Realize the positive energy that can emanate from your newly found niche.

- Enhancing your credentials enables you to increase your career options and marketability and broadens your horizons.

- Volunteer work is a knowledge and skill builder. Contributing your services as a volunteer often gives you more in the way of skills and knowledge than you can give.

Your Turn for Questions

- What do you need to focus on to find your niche?

- Do you feel you are in the right niche at this time? If so, how do you manage to keep it upbeat in the face of challenges?

- If you feel you need to make a change in the direction you're taking, what's keeping you from doing so?

- What would be the benefits of changing the direction of your life?

- Do you currently have enough control of your life to find your niche? If not, what's keeping you from having enough control?

- What do you do when negative forces try to dispel your seeking your niche?

- To this end, what else can be done that you're not doing now?

- How could changing your direction help to enhance your credentials?

- Do you currently volunteer your time or energy? If not, why not?

- What do you think you could gain from volunteering your time?

5

Think Big

Thinking big is moving beyond solely being an employee and a consumer. It also entails focusing on owning and controlling a share in America. Everyone has the potential to move beyond the limitations of a single source of income; what is needed is the development of the habit of thinking big. If all you think about is getting and holding a job, you are probably not on the path to becoming rich. Someone who has been conditioned to think on a small scale will have difficulty thinking big. To safeguard yourself against recession, offshoring and job separation, you're going to have to think about getting off a salary treadmill.

Now is the time to move beyond being solely an employee and a consumer. Many have the potential to become self-employed, but because most people have not been systematically exposed to such opportunities or they're discouraged in the educational process, many would-be sole proprietors spend their lives disgruntled as they punch the clock.

Most people spend their salaries as quickly as they earn them. They are not flush with money, and when it's time to retire, they are likely to have problems managing money throughout their lifetime. A person working for forty-five years at a fairly good salary will have earned $3 million in a lifetime. He or she would have had to have earned about twice the amount and supplemented it with a business or a series of profitable investments to be able to have comfortable years ahead. The reward is seeing your wealth grow and retiring at an age young enough to enjoy it.

A recent study painted a more pessimistic picture of the finances of pre-boomer and older boomer households. It reported a significant drop in median wealth among households headed by people ages forty-seven to sixty-four in 1998, compared with households in the same age group in 1983.[1]

As an employee, you may have been conditioned to think only in the narrow sense of getting your job done. At the end of the day, while you have the satisfaction of knowing that you've done what you are paid to do but no more, you haven't done anything different than what you did the day before or the day before that. To begin to think big and achieve the wealth you need to become financially independent, you must begin to think outside the box when it comes to your career. While on the job, think long and hard about the boss and the business. What might you do differently if you ran the company? Every day, we are in situations that could be improved. Thinking big means not just noticing where improvement is needed, but also coming up with possible solutions.

Most of the affluent in America are business owners, including self-employed professionals. These people do not have to follow orders or observe working hours set by someone else. It provides them with the opportunity to prove what they can accomplish.

Two widely reported studies from Rand Corporation and the Brookings Institution found that individuals typically become rich not from inheritance but by maintaining their health and working hard. Most of their savings comes from earnings and has nothing to do with inherited family wealth.[2]

How is it possible for people from modest backgrounds to become affluent in one generation? These affluent people had to have the courage to take control of business opportunities that were associated with considerable effort. Most ventures began as an idea, and although the public may often think of business only in terms of big business, they may not remember that most of the big corporations in this country started out as small businesses or ventures, a classic example is Bill Gates and Microsoft.

Consider these suggestions for stretching yourself and thinking big that can help you attain financial independence:

Determine how you can uncover your hidden talents. Many people feel that they are not creative enough or talented enough to succeed in what they want to do. In fact, your creative activity and talents are limitless, as long as you put them to use. It's not how talented you are, but how you are talented that really matters. You can discover this by taking any number of aptitude tests to uncover what talents you have that remain hidden from view. You may discover that you have talents that have been hidden even from yourself and therefore do not get developed. Too many people have a tendency to feel they do not have talents that they have.

Determine how you can build a venture that will grow; you can have an investment or build a business that will make money for you, even though you are not working at it full-time. Also, it helps when you are doing what you are passionate about. Making your money work for you means that you can take on bigger ideas and wealth-building projects.

Experiences to Learn From

I was aware that if my road map only included staying on a job, as good as it might be, financial independence would not likely be the result. After talking with an American friend on vacation in Paris while on my Fulbright scholarship about his Wall Street job and bonuses he made as a trader with Goldman Sachs, I decided it was time for me to think big and find a way into the lucrative business of Wall Street.

Seeking a position as a trainee with an investment firm like Goldman Sachs was not a likely prospect for me in the early 1960s. Returning to New York, I arranged an appointment with the Securities and Exchange Commission and uncovered a not-widely-known way in which I could become a licensed broker-dealer and market investments directly to clients through my own business. First, I would need to go through the NASD screening: interviews, questionnaires, and exam. After completing this process, which took me several months, I became licensed by the NASD as a general securities principal of my broker-dealer firm. I submerged myself in the voluminous rules and regulations of the industry. I also needed to understand the needs of my prospective client base and develop an effective method of condensing the data and presenting it in a clear and concise manner to enable prospects to make smart investment decisions. My day job as a teacher continued, and after school I met with my clients. Within several months, word-of-mouth referrals were giving me an increasing number of new prospects, and my venture was gaining incrementally.

I saw firsthand how much behind-the-scenes work it takes in this business to be successful. Each client, as per NASD rules, had to receive a prospectus for each program that was being offered. The NASD rules also required detailed record-keeping to have readily available for audit purposes at any time. Many of the systematic investment programs being purchased by my clients were for ten-year or fifteen-year durations and as a new company, I could be audited twice a year. The securities business is the most highly regulated industry in the United States.

It takes considerable confidence to work in an environment in which one is only compensated according to one's performance. My first year was a banner year—with eighty-hour working weeks and a great sacrifice of all of my discretionary time and with an increasing number of clients who wanted to make appointments with me. Sales exceeded $1 million. I had identified a new market, initially referred to me by friends and relatives. I became aware that I had uncovered an untapped reservoir of investors, often looking for a way to share in the American dream. They became my client base.

This community consisted of mostly middle-income families, often with two breadwinners, who wanted security, homeownership, and college education for their children. To provide this, they came to realize that they had to have some of their hard-earned money invested and working for them. Their business was not being courted by Wall Street firms. These clients were ready to proceed with investment strategies, and they had confidence that I would be there to service their investment needs. I was positioned to tackle this market with an enormous potential for growth.

My company, which was later incorporated as Creative Investor Services, Inc., has serviced clients for over forty years, marketing securities, insurance, and real estate products including syndications. I cherish my certificate of achievement award received five years ago which reads: "For 40 years of continued growth and customer satisfaction, 1962–2002."

Tips

Tip 1. *You are more likely to become rich and financially independent if you do not limit yourself to just the income from a single job.*
It is important to consider all of the options you have if your goal is to become rich. I built my fledging business while teaching and realizing income from two revenue streams.

Tip 2. *Determine what knowledge you possess that can lead you to financial success.*
Seek out areas that you are familiar with so that you can productively help others meet a need that they realize they have at the same time that you achieve your goal of a profitable business. I contacted people from the community I was working with—hardworking, ordinary people: postal workers, schoolteachers, civil service workers, to mention a few—who became my client base.

Summing Up

• Many affluent people in America acquired their wealth on their own. They had to have the courage to undertake entrepreneurial and other business opportunities that were associated with considerable efforts.

• You will be more likely to acquire financial independence if you do not limit yourself to a single source of income. It is important to consider all of the options that you have if your goal is to become wealthy.

• Determine what talent you possess that can lead you to financial success. Seek out areas that you are familiar with so that you can help others meet a need that they have.

Your Turn for Questions

• Are you willing to make serious changes in how you are working and living today?

• What second job would you take today if you could?

- What might that say about you?

- What areas of specialty do you have that could benefit your peer or social community?

- How might you go about leveraging those skills?

- Who would your clients be in such an endeavor?

- What business opportunity would you engage in?

6

Manage Fear

Life is either a daring adventure or nothing.
Helen Keller (1880–1968),
author and activist

Sometimes people do not pursue a great opportunity because of fear. Hesitating is sometimes a camouflage for not taking the opportunity to make a legitimate change. Fear of change, while clinging to outmoded systems, may ultimately block you from achieving your primary goals. Don't let fear bog you down from doing what you want to do. Consider what you need to do to keep you moving ahead as you would like to; examine what is creating stress for you and draining your energy, and study where your weaknesses are affecting what you are trying to achieve.

One of the biggest fears people have that inhibits them doing something they want to do, such as starting their own business, is fear of being ridiculed over a failure. They can be afraid and act anyway. Successful self-employment is only possible when one has learned to manage fear. Pushing through fear can stretch people, expand them, and truly enhance their lives. The cure for fear is to push ahead with what frightens them, if they can.

The ultimate objective is not to be susceptible to the multitude of fear-based errors that come from rationalizing and subconsciously distorting information. Eliminating fear is only half of the equation; the other half is hard work, preparation, and perseverance. However, those planning to try self-employment should be aware that longer hours, unsteady income and uninspiring statistics for success are likely.

When self-employed, you must be able to motivate yourself, because being on your own means you are assuming the risk of failure. Working for yourself rather than an employer and earning and directing your own livelihood puts the reliance upon you to deliver the profits or suffer the losses. If you want to be successful, you will have to conquer your fears and make the decision to take the risk. You must develop the ability to ignore or get past the fear of making a mistake. As an individual, you learn that it is important to acquire a mental structure that allows you to overcome your fear by building up your internal strengths and finding ways around your weaknesses.

Almost half of the workforce in the United States is employed by small businesses. After agonizing over all the possibilities of what could happen as a result of going into business on their own, most successful business owners have plowed ahead. You can be one of those business owners.

The primary purpose for exploring self-employment is to be able to realize the fullest potential available and be able to control your time, control your money, and control your life. Self-employment means being more independent, realizing tax advantages, and having a potentially flexible schedule. Being self employed also compels a person to continuously stimulate their mind.

The best way to master the fear of self-employment is to forge ahead regardless of the difficulties of long hours, fatigue, and building a clientele. This kind of challenge is not for everyone. To make it work, you need to dream big and have the energy to work tirelessly toward your goal. Not everyone is suited to be self-employed or an entrepreneur. Before plunging into uncharted waters, you need to know if you possess the necessary qualities. One key to success is to maintain a positive attitude.

Experiences to Learn From

When I first started out as a self-employed NASD broker-dealer providing investment advice and investment products to clients, I was still employed as a high school teacher. At the time, I did not know how long I would be able to do both to my satisfaction. Two primary risks were that the investment of time and money would take years to show a profit, and that developing my side business could potentially have adverse effects on my day job. I soon realized that selling had become a passion of mine, and I enjoyed the one-on-one interaction with my clients, some of whom I got to know very well. To my surprise and delight, my client base grew exponentially. Approaching marketing from the customer's perspective reaped rewards. By visiting the homes of prospective clients and listening to their situations and their aspirations, I acquired the necessary knowledge to fashion a match between what they needed to be able to create wealth and the benefits they would derive from selected investments.

Some of my "fifty-plus generation" clientele that I was reaching had vivid memories of the great stock-market crash of 1929 and the ensuing Great Depression. At the same time, they were aware of fortunes being made by stock-market investors. They had to be assured that they could do much better through carefully selected high performing investments than they could do through traditional bank savings accounts. However, time and the success that I was experiencing were too much for me to handle alone. I would not be able to continue as a one-man band for long, as the increase in my client base would not allow me the time to continue to service the growing number of prospects. I needed a sales team.

I turned to a few Wall Street professionals that I knew for insight into securing registered reps that could join me in addressing this market. What became apparent was that there was no reservoir of licensed reps for me to draw from, and I quickly realized that I would have to recruit, train, and develop my own personnel, a move that would help others gain a foothold in the securities business. I began a drive to find prospects for the company's growth under the new name of Creative Investor Services, Inc.

The prospect for success was not encouraging, and a few broker-dealers, when they learned of my ambitious plan to recruit and train my own sales force from scratch, doubted that it could be successful. In the face of these discouraging reactions, I had to reassure myself that this was definitely possible and overcome my apprehension that this was the right move for my business at that time.

I set my goal to have fifty registered reps as part of my company within a five-year period. Finding people who were committed to my blueprint and equipping them to be productive was my challenge. I only set three primary criteria for candidates to become registered reps: a compelling drive to be successful, strong self-esteem, and an ability to handle rejection.

My early clients were from urban areas, but many of my later clients were from the suburban and outlying areas. My sales force came from many of the same communities. By forging ahead, I was able to build up the sales force to handle the workload. The outcome was the growth of Creative Investor Services, which in time caught the eye of *The New York Times* and numerous other publications around the country.

My business had uncovered a market that had not been courted by Wall Street. There was a reservoir of discretionary funds that were held in low-interest savings accounts that were transferable into investments. It had not been difficult for me to realize the million-dollar sales in my first year, partly because I was not facing any competition from the Wall Street community. These companies doubted that there were any substantial funds held by inner-city residents that merited the investment of their time and effort. It was not until *The New York Times* highlighted my successes six years later in their financial section that some brokerage firms became aware of this previously untapped reservoir of capital and initiated a marketing effort to capitalize on it.

Tips

Tip 1. *Master your fears.*
Mastering your fears will open new vistas. When I decided to start a business in a field that was new to me and in a highly regulated industry, there were those in the business community that doubted my success. I was a bit apprehensive, but conquering this fear reaped unimaginable dividends.

Tip 2. *Self-employment can offer you more opportunities for financial independence, creativity, and expansion.*
Developing your business idea could enable you to structure an environment where you have control over your destiny. By becoming self-employed, I achieved an exciting amount of freedom limited only by my own initiative.

Tip 3. *Recognize that self-employment is challenging and risky but rewarding.* Understanding the challenges, risks, and rewards of self-employment will motivate you and increase your likelihood of success. I devoted a great amount of effort to my second career while continuing to work full-time.

Tip 4. *Continue to find customers and meet their needs.*
Finding and satisfying customers' needs are a fundamental process that results in customer satisfaction. My contacts with prospects revealed customer needs that selective investment programs were able to satisfy.

Tip 5. *Overcome hurdles and obstacles.*
Don't be overly influenced by naysayers. I had to ignore negative attitudes of some professionals who expressed their doubts about my ability to recruit and train sales personnel.

Tip 6. *Know your market.*
Unrealistic expectations can lead to failure when expectations do not meet with the reality of the market. I knew that there was a sizeable market that no one was servicing.

Summing Up

- Smart people don't let fear stop them, because they know that fear is a crippling emotion. Fear of being ridiculed over failure is often the biggest fear people have regarding starting their own businesses. Successful self-employment is only possible when you have learned to manage fear.

- Working for yourself rather than an employer and earning and directing your own livelihood puts the impetus on you to deliver the profits or suffer the losses. You can't allow the fear of making a mistake to inhibit you. The ultimate objective around this fear is not to be susceptible to the multitude of fear-based errors. Mastering your fear will open new vistas.

- Self-employment can offer you more opportunities for financial independence, creativity, and expansion. Developing your business idea could enable you to structure an environment where you have control over your destiny.

- Recognize that self-employment is challenging and risky but rewarding. Understanding the challenges, risks, and rewards of self-employment will increase your likelihood of success.

Your Turn for Questions

- What are your fears about striving to achieve success?

- What inspires or contributes to these fears?

- Are these fears grounded in real concerns? If so, what can be done to address these issues? If not, why do you think these fears persist?

- Who do you feel would be the biggest critics of your efforts toward success?

- Conversely, who would be your greatest supporters or advocates?

- What could you do to ensure the support of these advocates in your endeavors?

- If you could conquer your fear of failure, what goals do you think you could realize?

- How would you feel if you accomplished those goals?

- Do the benefits of success feel as if they would outweigh concerns about potential setbacks?

- What one thing could you do right now to begin managing your fear of moving forward in your life?

- What are you waiting for?

7

Self-Employed or Entrepreneur? There Is a Difference!

In my factory we make cosmetics, but in my stores we sell hope.
Charles Revson (1906–1975),
American founder of Revlon Cosmetics, Inc.

Someone who earns a living working for someone else is an employee of that business. There are many different types of employees, but they all share one thing: their labor is going into building someone else's business and wealth. Often, people dream of owning their own business and being their own boss with the prospect of making big money, but many hesitate to take the plunge. They worry that they don't have enough money, smarts, or experience to start and operate their own business. Once you have overcome these worries, it is time to think like the self-employed person or entrepreneur you may become.

Entrepreneurship is the American dream. Many people, however confuse being self-employed with being an entrepreneur. The difference is little understood; a self-employed person works by himself and for himself and has to be able to motivate only himself, while an entrepreneur organizes, operates, and assumes the risks of a business and hires people to whom he delegates the work. The man who buys paints and paintbrushes and does the manual work of painting your home himself is self-employed. The man who buys a van or pickup truck and then hires a slew of people to do the manual work of painting your home, sets up an LLC or files corporation papers, and is responsible for payroll, workers' compensation, insurance and social security taxes and maybe health insurance is an entrepreneur: a business owner to whom others answer. Successful business owners tackle problems and develop the practices that will work for them. They take the responsibilities for success or failure, and they realize the results.

The successful entrepreneur is ultimately dependent upon his ability to lead. Being an effective leader means being able to work with people who have differing skills and being able to get those you work with to optimize their skills and talents so that they can be successful in achieving the goals you set for your company. Being successful as an entrepreneur, you will need to have leadership qualities, including problem-solving ability, inventiveness, and the ability to delegate authority. Most importantly, a successful entrepreneur has the ability to think in terms of long-term goals and a capacity for hard work. Leaders have the function of clearing the path toward the goals of the group by meeting the needs of subordinates. Using the metaphor of a conductor of an orchestra illustrates leadership. The leader has to somehow get a group of potentially diverse and talented people, many of whom have strong personalities, to work together toward a common goal. There is however, a distinction between a leader and a manager. Leaders primarily concern themselves with people, while managers mainly concern themselves with tasks.

Entrepreneurs must possess certain personalities and character traits. They must be assertive, bold, and courageous. Optimism and the willingness to take controlled risks are important. They must be adaptable, flexible, and able to cope with changing situations, but they must also be organized, efficient, and decisive. To be a successful entrepreneur, you must be sure of yourself and your competition. It helps to be able to handle all types of personalities, especially those that don't necessarily agree with your own. It is important to center your business on something that you want to do and are gifted at. You may be working at it for sixty to eighty hours or more a week, so you need to be excited to get to work to ensure success.

Everyone's goals must be their own. Being an entrepreneur is not for everyone. For many people, the American dream is to have a great job and not have their own business. Many people are content to accommodate to the environment they're in rather than to control it. Entrepreneurs however, try to take control of their destinies rather than being controlled by them.

Entrepreneurs are optimists who see opportunities where others see problems. The most important preparation an entrepreneur needs for success is knowledge of the marketplace. To be successful an entrepreneur needs to identify what consumers need and want to buy. Some entrepreneurs recognize a consumer's need that consumers themselves don't see immediately until a marketing campaign is launched.

Becoming a successful entrepreneur also depends upon the ability to finance the enterprise. Banks generally won't risk lending money to start-up businesses, however sometimes entrepreneurs can secure personal loans from family and friends. Some people adapt to the demands of becoming an entrepreneur by spending their off hours working for additional income before stepping out on their own and launching their own company.

Many immigrants become entrepreneurs. They face many challenges, including learning a new language and new customs. Some have little money to start with, and they are willing to work eighteen-hour days, seven days a week to get a piece of the American dream. Immigrants often see opportunities where others, who are familiar with the country they are born in, do not. In a sense, they are forced by circumstances to become entrepreneurial. Perhaps this is why so many immigrants to the United States have started their own small businesses.

By definition, business is the buying and selling of products and services in order to make money. Starting and running a business can be one of the fastest tracks for wealth building, but it can be very hard work to get off the ground. You will need to know everything you can know about any business that you are considering starting. However, if you are launching a start-up business on your own and are relying on your fledging business to pay your bills from the beginning, you are going to fail. People who tend to fail go into business for passion, without a fallback, cash flow, or preparation for trials and tribulations. When difficulties come, these business owners are below where they started, and it dehumanizes them and makes them feel like failures. Having backup resources from family or the ability to get loans is a necessary preparatory step to prevent the fall.

With the proper motivation, there is often time to start your own business, even if you hold a full-time job. If you always wanted to own your own business and have the dream and the desire but don't have the capital or the knowledge, you may want to seek a position in a related field, make the money that you need, and begin to develop the plans that you need to move into the business that you have chosen.

Once you determine what sort of business you want, consider whether to buy an already-existing company or start one from scratch. Both options have advantages and disadvantages. An ongoing business will have all of its operating systems in place but may be more costly than starting your own. Starting from scratch can be a scary option, but the initial costs are often not as high since you pay neither a seller or for a franchise. Individuals who succeed with their own ideas shape every aspect of their businesses, from selecting a company name to deciding on a corporate structure and location.

Experiences to Learn From

This chapter tells the story of how an unlikely business grew within an untapped market by overcoming one hurdle after another and finally developing a crash course to successfully train fifty men and women to become NASD registered reps, enabling them to sell investments through a first-of-its-kind African American–owned Wall Street broker-dealer firm. The growing company pried open the door for African American reps and their clients so that they could enter a field that had not been opened to them and explore and develop new markets that had been untapped in the early 1960s. I had great success convincing a growing number of people to invest in the stock market through my firm. Underlying the story was the issue of a missed opportunity within the bastion of the free-enterprise system that Wall Street represented.

I ran ads in local papers, and within a month, I received dozens of responses, showing that there were many people willing to sign on for a second career with my broker-dealer firm. Over the next few weeks, I selected six candidates for my first training class. The first group was made up of men and women who showed potential for passing the difficult NASD Series 7 exam. They had solid education and work experience but wanted more.

The first meeting of the group was devoted to covering what their mission was, an orientation to the business of sales, and an overview of what they would be offering their clients if they were successful in the licensing examination.

The primary aim of each trainee was to pass the Series 7 exam. The NASD required a passing grade of 70 percent to become licensed. That meant a commitment to classes and mountains of homework. Those who were successful knew that they would earn a sizeable commission for any investment products they sold. They were highly motivated.

I used the ensuing months to develop and customize a series of training materials. This first class was made up of two real estate salesmen, an electrical engineer, a medical technician, a postal worker, and a homemaker. I developed programmed instructional modules together with problem-solving manuals for homework, with heavy emphasis on the quantitative units that students and trainees often gloss over. They learned how to analyze questions before answering them, and we had a series of dry-run exams each week on the modules that we had covered to test their exam-taking skills. This group spent many grueling hours studying. They studied NASD rules and regulations and the details of common stock, preferred stock, government bonds, debentures, open-end and closed-end investment trusts, disclosure requirements, and much more. At the end of the four weeks of classes, everyone took a two-hour preexam under exam conditions, and I reviewed each exam with them individually. For those who passed the preexam, I immediately scheduled the NASD exam for the next week. The results were astounding. Everyone who passed the preexam test also passed the NASD exam.

The commitment to the business would take these reps away from family and friends during the hours when most people would be seeking leisure from the week's toil. In addition, they had to be highly motivated and able to handle rejection and bounce back to be successful in the challenging field of sales. All reps signed an agreement with Creative Investor Services detailing their responsibilities and providing them with the schedule of commission payments.

After they passed the NASD exam, my challenge was to devise a course that would turn the newly licensed recruits into salespeople. I designed a brand-new sales-training program that zeroed in on those factors that affect sales, with drills on the fundamentals. I wanted to give them the best techniques available. Once the selling techniques were covered and they had the lessons and reading materials to perfect their technique, we moved to the ABCs of selling investments. First, they were directed to determine the prospect's investment objectives: education, retirement, tax shelter, and future income. These included meeting a prospect properly, preplanning a presentation, using the telephone effectively, handling objections, and defeating feelings of failure. These are but a few of the many modules we focused on in our sessions on selling investments. We were turning need for more income and more security into something else even more important: taking more control of their lives, becoming more inner-directed and not simply taking the easiest course of moving along with the tide.

I structured role-playing practice exercises between sales reps and customer to make the transition to their new career easier so that the new reps could see themselves in a situation, correct errors, and gain the needed confidence. I added modules that dealt with how to prospect, how to qualify your prospective customer, and how to close.

And then came the most important lesson of all: how to close a deal. I learned this early in my career, and I imparted it to my recruits. After the closing question, *shut up*! In other words, whenever you ask a closing question, stop talking. The first person to speak *loses*. This is much harder to do than it sounds, and it takes practice. I encouraged each of them to remember this when they made an offer to a current or potential customer.

These new recruits were now newly registered reps, making their first successful sales and leaving with their commission checks tucked in their pockets. With all of the sales techniques under their belt, the differences between those who would succeed and prosper and those who would not make it was what I call the persistence factor—tenacity. I designed a recruitment brochure detailing the benefits in becoming a sales rep with Creative Investor Services.

In four years, the company had a sales force of registered reps, all licensed and producing. Some of the reps were part-timers, working for Creative Investor Services while continuing in their regular jobs. In time, I attracted a diverse group of recruits that included men and women, black and white, college graduates and non-college graduates. Each of *the* sales reps had gone the distance: study, hard work, and passing the securities exam before they could receive any compensation.

As part of my marketing strategy for the now-licensed reps' clients, I arranged investment seminars, often held at the Americana Hotel in New York. The seminar program, always filled with participants eager to learn, provided attendees with knowledge and information on investing. I included various investment short-cuts in my seminars such as the Rule of 72. This rule was a method of manually calculating, in precomputer days, the number of years it would take for an investment or savings account to double. By dividing the dividend or interest into the number seventy-two, you calculate the number of years it takes for your money to double. This simple tool was used to quickly help the attendees evaluate investment proposals. The new sales reps found the seminars very helpful in selling to their new crop of clients.

Many of my reps told me that they did not expect to be having a connection to Wall Street in such a short time. Most had little knowledge of the investment world beyond the Dow Jones reports that they heard on the evening news between the sports and the weather before joining Creative Investor Services.

I planned a visit to Wall Street for my new reps, and we toured the New York Stock Exchange with its controlled chaos and its ticker-tape strip rapidly blinking stock reports, then onto the office of Don Spiro the president of Oppenheimer Corporation, one of our affiliated investment companies.

From the very beginning, I realized that I would really enjoy not being dependent on anyone but myself for my job security. I wanted to make my own decisions, and I was prepared to accept the responsibility that those decisions would affect my bottom line. That's part of what being an entrepreneur means to me. Now that I have done it, I realize that the hard work of establishing and running a business not only reaped great financial rewards but enabled me to do the things that I was most passionate about. Although I faced obstacles and setbacks, I was able to move forward with my plans.

Since my decision to do it on my own, I have come to realize how many of us have problems taking the plunge into entrepreneurship or self-employment because the decision-making process often involves wanting success without knowing exactly how to proceed.

Tips

Tip 1. *A positive attitude, optimism, and self-esteem are three essential qualities of a successful entrepreneur.*
Demonstrating a positive attitude will increase your likelihood of success. These traits were crucial to energize salespeople who helped my company develop sizeable profits.

Tip 2. *Friends and acquaintances can help you make a great start for your business ventures.*
Starting with a familiar base makes it easier to launch a new venture. I derived a list of prospects from family and friends for my investment products.

Tip 3. *Leadership skills are essential.*
Sharpen your leadership skills so that you can work with various people to accomplish your goal. As an entrepreneur, when I had to recruit, train, and manage fifty representatives, having strong leadership skills was essential.

Tip 4. *Explore new markets.*
Expanding into a new market can be very profitable. Uncovering an untapped community's interest in investment products proved very profitable.

Tip 5. *Develop your product line.*
Identifying and selecting a product line that meets the specific needs of your prospective customers will enhance your likelihood of success. Utilizing company data to determine the likelihood of profitability for my customers was essential to our early success.

Tip 6. *Understand how to individualize and distinguish your service or product from your competition.*
Individualizing and restructuring your service or product to meet the needs of your clients will increase the likelihood of success. I segmented my client base and reviewed dozens of products before selecting a small number for each client grouping.

Tip 7. *Find people to work for you.*
As an entrepreneur, it is essential that you locate and motivate people willing and able to join you on the way to accomplishing your goal. I found people who were interested in selling securities through Creative Investor Services.

Summing Up

- Many people confuse being an entrepreneur with being self-employed. The difference is little understood—an entrepreneur organizes, operates, and assumes the risk of a business and hires people to whom he delegates the work; a self-employed person works by himself and for himself.

- Entrepreneurship is the American dream. Many people dream of owning their own business and being their own boss with the prospect of making big money, but many hesitate to take the plunge. They worry that they don't have enough money, time, smarts, or experience to start and continue their own business.

- By definition, business is the buying and selling of products and services in order to make money. Starting and running a business can be one of the fastest tracks for wealth building, but it can be very hard work to get it off the ground. You will need to know everything that you can know about any business that you are considering starting.

- If you are expecting a start-up business of your own to pay your bills from the beginning, you are going to fail. People who tend to fail go into business for passion, without a fallback, cash flow, or preparation for trials and tribulations.

- If you always wanted to own your own business and you don't have the capital or the knowledge, but you have the dream and the desire, you may want to seek a position in a related field, make the money that you need, and begin to develop the plan that you need to move into the field you have chosen.

- Once you determine what sort of business you want, consider whether to buy a company or start one from scratch. Both options have advantages and disadvantages. An ongoing business will have all of its operating systems in place but may be more costly than starting your own.

- Entrepreneurs are optimists who see opportunities where others see problems. The most important preparation an entrepreneur needs for success is knowledge of the marketplace. One of the goals of an entrepreneur is to figure out what can be sold that consumers need and want to buy. Some entrepreneurs recognize a consumer's need that consumers themselves don't see immediately until a marketing campaign is launched.

- Leadership is an essential component in being an entrepreneur. Being successful as an entrepreneur ultimately depends upon your ability to be a leader, and being an effective leader means being able to work with people that have differing skills.

- Initially, friends and acquaintances can give you a great start for your sales campaign. Starting with a familiar base makes it easier to begin to enter a new venture.

- Explore new markets. Expanding into a new market can place you on the fast track.

- Continue to find customers and meet their needs. Approaching marketing from the customer's perspective will reap rewards.

- Leadership skills are essential. Sharpen your leadership skills so that you can work with various people to accomplish your goal.

- Find people to work for you. It is essential that you locate and motivate people willing and able to join you on the way to accomplishing your goal.

- Overcome hurdles and obstacles. Don't be overly influenced by negative viewpoints.

- Optimism and self-esteem are essential qualities of a successful entrepreneur. Demonstrating a positive attitude will increase your likelihood of success.

Your Turn for Questions

- What kind of labor are you performing right now? Who is profiting from this work?

- Are you content to let someone else profit from your work, or would you rather be the primary profiteer from your efforts?

- Would you rather be an entrepreneur or self-employed? Why?

- If you were to start a company, the chances are great that you would not initially draw a profit. Do you have a source of funding that you could draw upon until your business became profitable?

- Would it be more advantageous for you to buy a company or start one from scratch? Why?

- What friends, relatives, or acquaintances could you draw upon to gain an initial list of prospective clients?

- What new markets might you explore in order to be a first in that field?

8

Capitalize on the Media and Publicity

If you give the consumer a snapshot where he could see himself as he really is and the way he wants to be portrayed, people really respond to it. That emotionalism translates into behavior in the marketplace.
Thomas Burrell (b. 1939),
founder of the largest African American–owned agency, Burrell Communication Group

Will you be ready for the media interview when your big break comes? Are you at this moment media trained enough, media savvy enough, poised and skilled enough to tell your story when a reporter or interviewer asks you questions about your company, product or services? What if you don't know how to bring your story to life? What happens to all those media opportunities and the eager viewers, listeners, and readers across the country and the world who want an inner view of you? These questions are especially important if the media, publicity, and press attention is unexpected. You need to be prepared to capitalize on it.

Once you capture the attention of the media, prepare yourself for the interview. First you need to have a newsworthy story. In the media, content is king. Media people are constantly on the lookout for new information and ideas of interest and importance to their readers and viewers. The headlines and the first paragraph are the most important. Feed them the angle of your story that will interest their audience so they will use your slant to fill-up their column or program. Most writers and reporters will write their story up in the way that most meets the needs of their audience.

Know how to answer key questions, and focus the information about yourself based upon where the information will appear. If you know in advance that the reporter is seeking information for his column or program about finance, focus your response to that area. If the interviewer is interested in pitching information about housing and real estate, be prepared to respond to the interview so that the audience will want to listen or read on.

The basic principles of effective execution are within the grasp of an ordinary business owner. A catchy angle on your business and effective communication of a newsworthy message can do the trick very well and at little or no cost. You should ask when they think they'll run the story. Radio and TV stations will generally call because they prefer to have you available to discuss your business.

Print interviews are much harder than broadcasts. A print interviewer can keep you chatting for hours, so be prepared to set the guidelines early so that you have more control. Radio interviews offer the opportunity to focus your message toward a particular audience, both demographic and psychographic. Television is the most challenging medium because of its reach. Being a visual medium, you'll want the audience to focus on your message rather than flashy attire, so be prepared to dress accordingly.

Most stories come from people contacting journalists, either face to face, on paper, by phone, and more increasingly, via e-mail. If you are representing a company or organization, discuss all requests for interviews with the public information department of your organization. Find out as much as you can about the interviewer and the organization he represents. If it's print media, find out in advance if there will be a photographer present and dress accordingly. Get to your interview early and spend time practicing your message. Remember, you are the expert on the subject at hand, so seize this time to shine.

When being interviewed, keep your answers short, keep your message simple but not condescending, try to avoid professional jargon, and don't rush into answering questions that you need to take a moment to think about. When you have covered your message, stop talking until the next question is asked. Remember your key points and move back to them in every single answer. If you can't comment on a point, emphasize what you *can* say, and never say, "No comment."

You are the only one who can pitch or promote your company, product, or service. One of the greatest marketing tactics to increase exposure for the product, services or invention lies in working with the media, doing successful interviews, and getting as much media publicity as you can. Using your fifteen minutes of fame the right way can make you a star if you are prepared and have the interview skills it takes. Will you be ready when the big break comes? Remember, nothing is truly off the record. Once notes are made, editors can use them. If the interview goes off track, ask for a break, a glass of water, or a visit to the restroom. Information cannot be used if you have not said anything.

Learn how to bridge the move to the next subject or message you want to get across. Practice the art of answering the question you want to answer. You may want to say: What's really important here? I think the question you're asking is … How do I answer a question in a way that gets across my point and that is fairly close to the agenda? So how do you benefit from all this? Come up with a new angle and tell a journalist about it, and you can grab all the free publicity you ever want.

Experiences to Learn From

Getting national publicity in *The New York Times* was the big opportunity that accelerated the pace toward my goals and altered my direction. The article about my company with my photograph appeared on the front page of the business section. It was a masterstroke of publicity. Although it was unsolicited and its timing was unexpected, the article caused a rush of activity when it hit the newsstands. Once you are out in the press, you are treated with added respect. People like to be associated with you when you and your business are taken seriously by the press.

How did my business methods come to be covered on the front page of the business section of the *Times*? About two weeks earlier, while attending a cocktail party at one of my neighbor's homes, I was introduced to one of the guests, and we started the usual cocktail-party chitchat. The conversation eventually grew more involved as we continued. At one point, he explained that he owned a public relations firm, and he was curious as to what I was doing.

I told him about the company I had founded that was making a mark in the world of finance by training a cadre of people who had been in dead-end jobs to enter the citadel of capitalism—Wall Street. As the evening moved on, I knew I had piqued his interest, and we talked more about my company. He seemed quite interested that I was involved in a pioneer venture in the world of finance.

My enthusiasm must have further sparked his interest, because he continued with more questions about the company. I told him that my clients were largely inner-city folks who were interested in financial planning, and I was developing a new and sizable market. We talked about how I built my company from scratch by recruiting and training new salesmen to take the NASD licensing exam and then training them to sell securities. Before we parted that evening, he asked me to call him the following Monday morning at his office at the Pan Am building in Manhattan. We exchanged business cards.

On Monday morning when I called him, his secretary put me right through to him. He told me that he had someone who wanted to meet me and that I should come to his office at noon the following day, Tuesday. I cleared my calendar and went down to see him. When I got to his office, he told me that Robert D. Hershey, Jr., a finance correspondent for *The New York Times* business section, would be waiting for me at a local restaurant just blocks from his office, and he gave me the address.

Hershey and I had a long conversation in which he asked questions about Creative Investor Services, my recruitment efforts, my activities in expanding the sales force of my investment firm, and about me personally. I talked about the problems that I first had in recruiting registered reps that forced me to create a training program as a way to staff the company. Building my company the old-fashioned way, from the bottom up, caught this journalist's interest. We talked for hours about what I had been doing with my company. From our discussion, I sensed that the newspapers, always looking for novel and interesting stories, would be very interested in the story of Creative Investor Services.

Hershey wanted photographs to go with the story, so we went to the *Times* office to take the photos. When we finished, I explained to him how busy I was at the time, with classes and commitments piling up and my business commitments. I felt I couldn't handle any publicity coming out at this time. He assured me that there would be no story without my first knowing about it and promised to call me before the story went to press. It was about 4:30 PM when we parted.

I had been taking a summer doctoral course in statistics with Professor John Waldron at the Fordham University Graduate School so that I could complete my preliminary coursework early and get a jump on the other matriculation requirements. About 9:00 AM the next morning, Wednesday, July 31, 1968, Professor Waldron entered our classroom and said that he had an announcement to make before class began. He smiled slowly and said, "Class, I think we need to take a moment to acknowledge a celebrity in our midst." He dramatically pulled out *The New York Times*. Although there had been no call from Robert Hershey, the story was on the newsstand. Professor Waldron separated the business section from the rest of the paper and held it up to the class. On the front page, center, above the fold, was a large picture of me. I was astounded. The class applauded.

Crash Course Creates Salesmen. This one single photo and article had the most profound effect on me and my business and sparked a tidal wave of media coverage and public appearances. The story covered my successful effort in recruiting and training new registered reps for my growing investment firm. That one story changed my life and career for the next thirty-five years. This publicity was an acknowledgment and an endorsement of my company and its development in its first six years. This story was picked up by many other publications, including the *Orlando Florida Star*, the *Chicago Tribune*, the *Richmond Times Dispatch*, and the *Cincinnati Enquirer*, as well as television and radio appearances, including the WOR *Stock Market Observer*. Many television program appearances and business offers followed the publications of the story in the New York Times with Westchester Business Journal and Finance Magazine interviews. This experience thrust me onto the national stage.

After my surprise passed and upon reflection, I realized that there was a compelling need for this type of story at that time. The vacuum of publicity in the mid-1960s about African American businesses desperately needed to be filled. I had played a role in filling the void. Without the assistance of a public-relations firm, I had to make certain that my responses to media questions and other correspondence that came my way would further my objectives and goals. Once I was in the spotlight, I worked diligently to project my company's image of professionalism and entrepreneurship.

Almost as gratifying as the *Times's* article and the media attention that followed were the numerous letters from perfect strangers who delighted in what I had been able to accomplish. The letters came from those who wanted to know how they could become a part of the organization and those who had an interest in Wall Street and in selling. Many were interested in taking the crash course or joining the company. They cited their interest in sales, hunger for new careers, and some dissatisfaction with their job or their accomplishments. The letters, calls, and articles flowed continuously after that, and it was clear that Creative Investor Services was the right fit for the times and for those who were seeking additional careers and interested in financial planning services.

Most of the coverage I received was about someone who put his theories into practice. The media was also quick to pick up the fact that my company had dispelled the myth that business could not be done in the black community. What began as an untapped market for me and my company soon became a nationally known story about the leading black-owned broker-dealer firm in the country. I also made note in interviews that while I might be doing something spectacular; credit also had to be given to others, like my team of registered reps and the community of investors that we were servicing.

Tips

Tip 1. *Know how to use the spotlight to your advantage.*
Skillfully managing the spotlight can lead you to other opportunities. I conveyed to the *New York Times* correspondent what I did to make my company a success. This publicity led to my being recruited for a Xerox management position.

Tip 2. *Anticipate additional media attention, and be prepared.*
Showing an awareness of the opportunities presented when in the spotlight and how to utilize them will further your goals. Once I was in the spotlight, I worked diligently to project my company's image of professionalism and entrepreneurship.

Tip 3. *Understanding the media's interests and timetables will help you avoid pitfalls and achieve your goals.*
The better you understand the media, the more useful the publicity will be for you. Although there was limited time for notification by the *Times*, I quickly understood their reason for early publication of the story.

Summing Up

- Establishing credibility is essential to your long-term success.

- The media is a very powerful tool, and few get to benefit from it.

- Stay focused on what's important. Showing discipline, focus, and the proper work ethic rather than becoming distracted will lead to more favorable results.

- You and your business may be in the spotlight, and understanding the media process will help you avoid pitfalls.

Your Turn for Questions

- How would you feel if a story about your current efforts was published today in a national newspaper?

- What effort could you make to improve your skills in media interviews? What could you do next week and in the next month?

- If you could commission a media story about the state of your business, what aspects would you want to highlight? What would you want to downplay or ignore?

- Most media attention is unanticipated. What could you do right now to prepare yourself and your reputation for eventual media coverage?

- If a reporter approached you with an angle for a story that was unfavorable to you, what could you do to compensate for this?

The Early Years: Winston Allen's alma mater, The High School of Music &
Art, New York, ca. 1950's.

DeWitt Clinton High School economics club meeting with its founder,
Winston Allen, ca. 1960.

Fulbright Scholarship grantees arriving in Caen, France, greeted by the mayor, 1961. The author is in the top photo, second row, third from right.

College Discovery Program, director Winston Allen, conducting a luncheon faculty meeting at Queensborough Community College, 1968.

New York Times, "Crash Course Creates Salesmen." Feature story about Winston Allen and his company, Creative Investor Services, 1968.

Creative Investor Services sales reps meeting with company's founder and president, Winston Allen, Americana Hotel, New York City, ca. 1968.

Creative Investor Services seminar with Oppenheimer Management Corporation presenter sitting to the left of Winston Allen, ca. 1968.

Creative Investor Services' client at seminar receiving stock performance
data from Winston Allen, ca. 1968.

FINANCE

DECEMBER 1969
VOL. 87   NO. 12

Up Allen's Alley. Many minorities lack economic power. One solution to their problem lies in education. Winston Allen, •••••••• founder and head of the black-owned and run Creative Investors Service, is well aware of this and is trying to whittle away at the educational gap between Wall Street and blacks.

First, he had to dispel the myth that business couldn't be done in black communities. So, in 1962, running a one-man show, he sold $1 million in mutual funds. "The money was there, especially in the case of civil service workers, but lack of knowledge about investing had bred distrust," says the articulate executive. "I used personal contact. Besides, I was selling mutual funds with proved records."

Now that he has a staff, Allen uses seminars to acquaint the people with the benefits of investing. He says the turnout is good.

His next problem was recruiting sellers. Most had some college education, but none had any appreciable experience in the brokerage business.

So Allen, a former teacher at City College, set up a home training

program. "We now run a four-week crash course with Saturday classes and a mountain of homework," he says. More than 35 of his students have passed the stringent NASD test for selling equities and become versed in the world of finance. As a result, Creative now offers other services, such as insurance.

But the soft-spoken, yet aggressive, Allen won't stop there. He says: "There are plenty of black entrepreneurs who don't have proper capitalization but who do have good business ideas. The field is virtually untapped." He believes small syndicates can be formed to finance these potentially profitable businesses.

Allen plans to expand to many other cities but wants to avoid the pitfalls of expanding too quickly. Currently, more than 90 per cent of his clients live in black communities, but he thinks integration of his firm will broaden its base and help in the long run.

Helping people make money while making it yourself is a happy but somewhat risky undertaking. Like most creative people, Allen makes it look easy.

Finance Magazine story, "Up Allen's Alley."

Xerox World, 1973.

Leesburg: A Xerox Commitment to the Development of Its People

By Mandi Harris

Research in Education

"Xerox has always had a commitment to people development," said Dr. Winston Allen. "This center is the ultimate. Here we have the opportunity to be the pioneers in industrial training."

And if Xerox is the pioneer, Allen could be called the wagon master. He is the Leesburg Center's manager of education research and development.

This department works side by side with the Rochester curriculum group and the Center's school managers. They decide what is to be taught, and Allen's group works out with them the best ways to teach it.

Allen and his staff are in-house experts on how people learn. They bring to the Center the latest know-how in behavioral science, research, curriculum and instructional technology. They determine the best method of instruction for particular courses, and provide structure for the training programs. "In other words," said Allen, "we define the best way to get the message across."

Very often that method is visual. It has been found that people learn best through seeing and doing. So interaction plays an important part in the Center's training programs. The

Dr. Winston Allen, Leesburg's manager of education research and development, heads a staff he hopes will pioneer in education technique.

octagon-shaped classroom is another innovation in education strategy, Allen said. It is based on the concept of give-and-take between the instructor and student, and between student and student.

"They learn from each other as well as from the instructor," he said. "The lecture process isn't as effective largely because the students play a very passive role. In our program they're very active. The more active the students are, the more they learn."

The very idea of a Leesburg Center—in which students from all over the country come to one place to pursue several disciplines—extends beyond the classroom by giving students a chance to see what is on the

other side of the fence, to learn to appreciate business disciplines other than their own.

"Through this interaction", said Allen, "the students become better aware of the direction of the company, which in turn fosters professional growth and development.

"Here we can test new teaching methods, new media, and new techniques for introducing multi-media into the curriculum. We can further develop and implement our own research designs to further enhance our training products. This center is second to none in capabilities and potential."

In its short existence, the Center has already been visited by interest groups ranging from Army training specialists to Harvard University professors. It's entirely possible, said Allen, that instructional techniques developed at Leesburg will eventually be adopted by traditional learning institutions.

"And we're working closely with several colleges and universities," he said, "with an eye toward developing accredited programs here for our own people—courses in business administration, educational technology and psychology."

Rank Xerox headquarters in Dusseldorf, Germany. Winston Allen in strategy meeting with Rank Xerox executives, 1976.

Rank Xerox headquarters in Dusseldorf Germany. Winston Allen with Rank Xerox executive discussing staff development strategies, 1976.

THE CONNECTICUT LAW TRIBUNE   MARCH 19, 1990

Beginner's Luck? The fledgling firm of **Collins & Evans** in Stamford has yet to win a jury trial in Connecticut, but it's shown it can make it in the Big Apple: The firm won a $3.5 million verdict this month in a securities conversion case in New York State Supreme Court in Manhattan.

BEHIND
THE BAR

"This is the kind of thing you go through your life thinking it'll never happen and then you luck into it," says **Kevin F. Collins** of the hefty award handed down March 6.

Collins, 32, who is licensed to practice in New York as well as Connecticut, formed the law firm with **John J. Evans** three years ago after each had served associate stints with local attorneys. Collins says he concentrates in personal-injury law while Evans, also 32, focuses on commercial litigation.

Although most of their business is in Connecticut, Collins says having the dual admission "has really helped us through the lean years. New York

Collins cashes in—almost

attorneys will give me work in Connecticut and Connecticut attorneys will send me New York work," he says.

To bring home the $3.5 million verdict, Collins represented **Winston Allen**, a Westport real estate developer and securities dealer, against the John Murray House Cooperative Association in Manhattan. Collins successfully proved that the association's board had failed to transfer ownership of 14 percent stock in the co-op to Allen in a timely fashion, causing him to miss a significant business opportunity to resell the shares. Collins

says he believes the fact that Allen is black at least partly motivated the board's delay in signing over the stocks, which he borrowed approximately $2.2 million to purchase.

Allen says he turned to Collins & Evans because the firm had represented him in 1987 in a minor construction litigation matter and "did a very professional job." He also had recalled that Collins was admitted to practice in New York.

Collins says although he has had only one other jury trial—which he lost—since starting the firm, he expects more in Connecticut courts soon. "Our cases are going up the trial list, so it looks like we'll have more trials in the offing," he says.

But he wasn't so sure the firm would soon win another case of equal proportion. "It's not every day you win a three-and-a-half-million-dollar verdict," he laughs.

What *isn't* funny is that the firm did not take the case on a contingency basis—so Collins estimates the firm will earn only •••••• based on its billable hours instead of the more than $1 million it would have netted under the typical 33 percent contingency arrangement. To the big dollars lost, Collins stoically replies: "It's a judgment call."

—*Mark Walsh*

• • •

Connecticut Law Tribune article, "Behind The Bar."

Winston Allen inauguration as Rotary district governor, with Rotary International Vice President Abraham Gordon, 2000.

Rotary Foundation project team in South Africa. Author with wife, Ruby, in center of photo. Team leader, Rotary International Vice President Sonny Brown and wife, Ann, back row, left, 2001.

Cape Town Nozamo Day Care Centre Nursery School. The children are
showing off their skills in completing their puzzle to Rotary district governor Winston Allen and his wife Ruby in 2001.

Winston Allen inventor and wife, Ruby, at entrance to the Medi-Spa
Trade Show, Pier 94 New York City where his patented product, Hydro-
Tone was marketed, 2004.

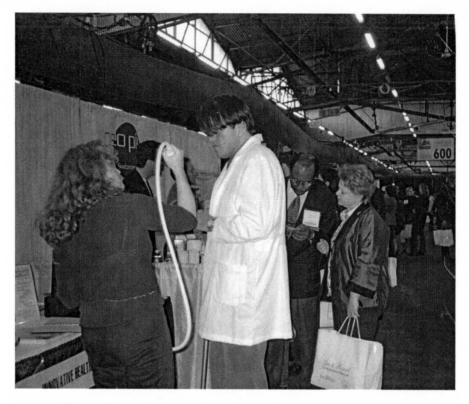

Visitors at the HydroTone trade-show booth experiencing the product, 2004.

9

Climb Aboard the Fast Track

The rung of the ladder was never meant to rest upon, but only to hold a man's foot
long enough to enable him to pull the other somewhat higher.
Thomas Huxley (1825–1895),
educator

Successful people look for the fast track to success. If the track you are on is not delivering the success you want, be prepared to change direction. To be prepared, you need to be able to make changes and at the same time keep your eyes open for opportunities. The plan you are following may not always deliver immediate benefits and gratification, but if you know that it is adding to your personal portfolio, stay with it. Successful people and successful corporations have a lot in common. They see challenges and not problems; they accept setbacks as temporary; and they live up to their highest expectations by making certain they get aboard the fast track. How do they do it? They avoid spending time on things that are not working. They are willing to change direction when it is called for. They know to watch for obstacles and navigate quickly around them. They don't waste time. They know how to be efficient with their resources. They have great introspection as to who they are and who they want to become.

In order for you to get on the fast track, you must decide between the path of greater security with a steady job and the path of greater risk by starting your own business. Successful business owners go for the fast track because it brings greater rewards—the reason for being in business. It is also important that people look for the opportunities when the time is right to accomplish the goals that they set for themselves.

How do you find the fast track contacts if you have just relocated? The most available resources are the business section of the local newspaper,

85

the Yellow Pages, and the Internet. In a matter of minutes, you can learn a great deal of important information about the businesses that interest you without leaving your home.

It is not enough to be in the right place at the right time. You have to be the right person in the right place at the right time. Don't be caught short with inadequate credentials either; this may limit you from taking advantage of opportunities to create wealth and financial independence.

Experiences to Learn From

Realizing that it was time for new challenges, I left my tenured position as a high school teacher to start work on a PhD pursuant to seeking a position on the college level. That move ultimately placed me on the fast track and landed me in corporate America as an executive with Xerox Corporation.

Before Xerox initiated plans to build a world class international training and management development facility, the company's business model showed that they needed to centralize their sales, service, and management development function and recruit a professional management team to restructure it, to keep pace with the company's unprecedented growth. Xerox was growing rapidly and went from $739 million to $8.5 billion in annual revenues in ten years, and the company became a business legend. The Xerox business model would have a profound effect on my plans and my professional career, because had these decisions not been made on the corporate level, my connection with Xerox would not have come about.

I had just completed my second year on the Fordham University faculty when my department chairman asked me if he could place my name on the search list for dean, as the current dean was retiring. A higher level within the college hierarchy would mean a much longer day and a much greater commitment than I was willing to make. I had my company to run, as well as personal and family commitments. I also knew that an administrative position in the university was not my long-range goal, as much as I enjoyed the camaraderie at Fordham and the intellectual stimulation it offered. I declined the offer.

In the midst of this crucial decision-making period, I got a call from an executive search firm that informed me that a Fortune 50 company was very interested in me. They wanted to talk with me. The executive search firm said. "They saw your article in the New York Times and what you were able to do with your company, Creative Investor Services. Think about this and call us back." In follow-up conversations over the next few weeks, I declined their suggestion to contact the company they were representing. I had more on my plate than I could handle. They kept coming back to me and said that the company wanted me to simply come in and talk with them. The company was Xerox. The search firm sent me a copy of the ad from Xerox that had appeared in *The New York Times* on January 2, 1972, for the position, that read, in part:

> Manager of Education Research and Development: starting salary plus profit-sharing plus stock options. Will be top educator at new multi-million-dollar training center to be located in Washington, D.C. area. Will have overall responsibility for education and training. Decided opportunities for advancement. Doctorate required.

I had already decided against accepting the deanship. I had a teaching schedule that allowed me more time to tend to my company. The ad was intriguing. If I were to seriously consider an American corporate position, it would mean restricting my plans to expand my business. This was a primary reason why I had not considered Fordham's possible offer of an administrative position; now I was beginning to think about a corporate position that would be far more demanding and would require relocation. I deliberated over my decision for the next few weeks and finally decided to at least go through the interview stage.

The Xerox meeting took place at their corporate headquarters in Stamford, Connecticut. The interviewers ushered me into the walnut-paneled conference room and promptly began by asking me to tell them how my background and capabilities prepared me for their position. I was asked to deal with some specific cases that were occurring at the company and what I would do in such situations. I answered their questions as candidly and succinctly as I could.

The meeting lasted about two hours. The next day, I received a call letting me know that the search team had decided that I was the right match for the position, and they wanted to move to the next step. Shortly afterward, I began to do some research on the company that was about to make me an offer. I knew from my research that Xerox was definitely on the fast track as the first photocopying company in America. The term *photocopying* soon became popularly known as *Xeroxing*, much to the chagrin of Xerox, who reminded everyone that the process was patented and their company's name was trademarked.

Training such a large number of sales and service employees was a major challenge for the company. They needed more effective and faster training methods. It was clear why Xerox Corporation was building an $80 million state-of-the-art training facility and was looking for someone with professional and business skills to head up the entire training and development function. Apparently, I was the person they were looking for: an entrepreneur with experience in training a sales force who had the doctoral credential they required.

I accepted Xerox's offer to visit their existing training site at Fort Lauderdale, Florida, as a consultant and give them my critique. A week later, I was on a plane heading for Fort Lauderdale with one of the Xerox executives. As it was midwinter, I was delighted to be heading south. When we got off the plane, the warm air contrasted sharply with the freezing weather we had just left behind. Having always loved bright, warm, sunny days, I felt I could really be motivated here.

The Xerox training school was housed on several floors of the Sheraton Hotel across from the beach. The Xerox executive and I agreed to meet at the restaurant for a snack after checking in. As we sat near the window eating lunch, there was a constant flow of traffic along the strip that separated us from the roar of the Atlantic surf, the beach, the sunbathers, and the volleyball games. This was the winter break for many colleges, and the beaches were filled with young women in bathing suits. The Xerox executive suggested that we might want to take off the afternoon and stroll along the beach before going to the training school. But I was more interested in learning what was ahead for me with Xerox than relaxing in the sun, as tempting as it was. It was only later that I learned how important my declining the offer was. As it turned out, there were reports to be submitted when we got back, and the statement was later made to me in jest that I had passed up a frolic on the beach for an afternoon in a classroom.

I spent the rest of the week in the classes evaluating their training methodology and the trainees' reactions to the process. There was very little I observed that I found effective for a company of Xerox's size. Trainees sat in rows, theater-style, with pencils, notebooks, and a trainer (one of the sales or servicemen) lecturing to them interspersed with a string of their successful "war stories." This type of training could not produce the results that Xerox needed and wanted. Their training methods needed a major overhaul to become effective, and I was scheduled to report my findings in Stamford upon my return.

Back in Xerox corporate headquarters in Stamford, I met with the top decision makers as well as the executive who had accompanied me on the trip to Fort Lauderdale. As I began my report that afternoon, the conference room was quiet as I presented my findings, conclusions, and recommendations. The only sound aside from my voice was their pencils against long yellow pads, taking notes. I detailed the shortcomings of the training program.

Sales training at Xerox at that time was not interactive but needed to be. Videotaped role-playing, an interactive tool for sales training, had not been utilized at Xerox. It was most essential so that sales staff could learn the techniques of handling customer questions and concerns. Also, salespeople needed to perfect and practice their techniques for selling benefits and meeting objections. In order to do this, a salesperson had to be able to identify customer needs. More than anything else, the sales professional needed to be able to read their prospective client's reactions and be able to adjust to them on the spot.

In my experience with Creative Investor Services, I found that successful sales personnel had certain qualities. They thrived on conquest and placing the order, getting the contract, and getting their intrinsic and extrinsic rewards. Some say that salespeople are born and not made. But I found that once I helped my reps in my company build up their sales skills, their confidence followed.

As in most companies at that time, Xerox training instructors during the 1960s were the company's super salesmen, the theory being that those with demonstrated sales ability could teach selling skills as well. I did not find that to be true; in fact, often the opposite was true. Also, this training method ensured that some of Xerox's best sales personnel were stuck in classrooms teaching rather than being in front of the customers selling and adding to the company's profits. I concluded my presentation by indicating that the Xerox training program, wherever it was conducted, needed a complete makeover.

I was offered the job of heading up the training and development function at Xerox. I turned down the offer of a full-time position at that time, but indicated I would consider continuing as a consultant as I was still on the faculty of Fordham, on a leave of absence. We agreed to meet in a week to finalize this.

With my decision about to be made, I checked out the details of the offer, weighed my options as I saw them, and talked to friends and family about my decision. Not surprisingly, I got several negative reactions: "You're in a very good position at Fordham." "American corporations are cutthroat, with no security." "Why subject yourself to the whims of a corporation?" These considerations, while they may have been valid, did not get to the nexus of the issue: this was an opportunity to enter a multi-billion-dollar corporation in a senior management position. I phoned Xerox a week later as promised and accepted their offer for a six-month period until I could wrap up my faculty position at Fordham.

We agreed on the terms, and I was given a set of offices at the Xerox temporary corporate headquarters at High Ridge Park in Stamford, Connecticut while the permanent corporate headquarters nearby was being completed, and we moved there. I immediately began to recruit a per diem staff of professionals who I knew would be able to begin systematically addressing the necessary changes in the Xerox training system. I insisted upon quality results, and I did not renew short-term engagements if production was not forthcoming.

For several months, my staff and I worked around the clock. At the same time, we had to adopt logical and operational strategies for responding to requests for training assistance from the field training groups. After setting goals for our group, I held out for tests in the field as a measurement of our effectiveness.

During that period, in addition to a complete overhaul of the way training was done at Xerox, I instituted the first formal teacher-training program. This new area I called "Train the Trainer," which provided a crash course in training methodology. Keeping with my philosophy of continuing education, teacher trainers and trainees received home-study modules for training in the classroom and use on the job. Trainers would no longer spend classroom time lecturing to their trainees and telling about their own experiences. Instead, they would give the trainees an opportunity to develop their sales skills and techniques in order to close the deal.

Within four months, I was finished with my summer project with Fordham, and Xerox immediately made me an offer for a full-time management position heading up Xerox's education, research and development function. Everything was occurring very quickly. Fordham found a replacement for me for the coming school year, and I accepted the position together with start-up arrangements, a budget for a staff, consultants, and expenses. The most important concession for me that Xerox made was their written agreement to accede to my request to keep my company, Creative Investor Services, operational while employed at Xerox.

Within weeks of taking the job, I pulled together a permanent staff of professionals who were able to get the training restructuring introduced throughout the corporation. I devised the overall strategy, including the process for training sales and technical personnel. The thirty professionals that I recruited and hired were equipped to do curriculum development, instructor training, audiovisual technology, and curriculum evaluation.

This was a great asset to me because the Xerox training facility was in the final stages of completion, and I had committed to having the program in place when the new facility opened. Many of the people that I hired came from earlier professional relationships, and I knew that they could get the job done.

On one occasion, I ran an ad that read:

> *Curriculum Evaluation, Design and Development for Xerox Educational Center*
> Xerox Corporation is committing major resources to its new International Center for Training and Development—a completely self-contained living/learning complex that will serve company-wide needs for the professional development of sales personnel, technical service representatives, managers and executives ... Requires Masters or higher degree, preferably in curriculum development, and 6 or more years' academic and industrial experience developing curriculum of the types indicated. The openings are immediately available and will be located initially in Stamford, Connecticut, with permanent location later this year at the new Center in Northern Virginia, 30 miles from Washington. Very fine salaries plus exceptional benefits. Write in confidence and in detail to Dr. Winston Allen, Education Research and Development, Xerox Corporation, International Headquarters, High Ridge Park, Stamford, Connecticut, 06904.

I received more than seven hundred résumés in a two-week period. I read through the résumés, held interviews, and hired additional professionals. Some of my staff and I traveled between Stamford corporate headquarters and the Fort Lauderdale training facility, and later to the new Leesburg training facility in Virginia. Once it was operational, I moved to my new offices there.

We made the interactive component the keystone of the sales training program and instituted videotaped role-playing of each trainee. The in-the-round classroom put trainees in a circle so that everyone could face each other eye to eye. In small groups we put the salesmen on camera, recorded both sound and picture on videotape, and then played the presentation for immediate evaluation. In this way we would know their progress and they would come to learn exactly what a first-class sales presentation should be like. Finally, all training programs were to be regularly evaluated for performance results.

These innovative changes that were met with skepticism at first by both the Fort Lauderdale school and the Rochester training group were soon beginning to be embraced, because the evidence of the improved field results of the new system was becoming apparent. This became even stronger after the audit that was commissioned by Xerox headquarters expounded upon the beneficial results of the new training methods. The newly instituted program was deemed a great success by the Xerox Learning Systems. The Xerox evaluators decided that we had built the necessary skills into the Xerox International Center for Training and Management Development.

Xerox totally controlled the copier/duplicator business in the early 1970s. It was clear to upper management that if they were going to take full advantage of their monopoly, sales reps had to place more machines in the field and the technicians had to repair them quickly. In the early years, Xerox only leased their copiers and duplicating machines; clients were billed according to the number of copies they made. A Xerox machine that could have been placed but wasn't affected the revenue, and a machine that needed repair was not adding to the bottom line. Xerox technicians had to be equipped to handle any repair problem when they were called upon. A well-trained sales and service force was critical to the company's growth.

While the Xerox center was under construction, I was involved with the design of the facility, primarily the octagonal shape of the classrooms to better accommodate the interactive curriculum. The state-of-the-art high-tech center, which opened in June of 1973, was on a 2,265-acre site and had facilities for one thousand students at any one time.

On June 2, 1973, *Xerox World* dedicated an entire issue to the Leesburg Center that was very supportive of our program. In part, the *Xerox World* article read:

> "Xerox has always had a commitment to people development," said Dr. Winston Allen. "This center is the ultimate. Here we have the opportunity to be the pioneers in industrial training." And if Xerox is the pioneer, Allen could be called the wagon master. He is the Leesburg Center's manager of education research and development. This department works side by side with the Rochester curriculum group and the Center's school. (See Appendix for full article.)

To assess the success of my operation and its innovative approach, an audit was ordered by Xerox CEO, Peter McColough, and conducted by Xerox Learning Systems (XLS). Tom Blodgett, a senior XLS executive at Xerox, conducted the extensive and detailed audit of my entire operation and my approach to training and development. Xerox wanted to be certain that they had invested in the right approach, and my strategy for training thousands of Xerox people. My group's professionalism and exceptionally strong performance in meeting the training needs in a timely manner was a critical factor in establishing our program companywide. The audit, dated March 1973, called our program "very successful." This was great news for my staff, because it meant that we had effectively transformed Xerox training that would now be institutionalized. The audit read, in part:

> Win has been attempting since he joined us to tackle, on all fronts, the sales training supports needs of ISG. The major topical areas we covered included Win's general approach as a resource to ISG, accomplishment to date, responsibilities in the immediate future, the organization he is putting together, and his charter in relation to the Leesburg Center Corporate Training in general ... When Win joined us last May and was faced with a number of requests for assistance (particularly because he was set up as an expert), he had to adopt certain strategies for responding to requests that were logical and operational. In general, he sought to understand the needs, set up a team, conduct a series of observation sessions, come to a group judgment, set targets, perform the work, test the results, and deliver.

As the audit circulated, it legitimized the investment that Xerox had made. It quickly led to greater requests for my operation throughout the company. In 1975 my responsibilities were expanded and I was relocated to corporate headquarters in Stamford, with a broader international assignment to promote the new training strategies, which continued into the 1980s. This assignment took me to Rank Xerox in Europe, the Palo Alto Research Center in Stanford, California, Scientific Data Systems (SDS) in Dallas, Texas, and other Xerox operations.

In the early 1980s, American corporations were adopting sharp cost-cutting budgets and reducing power on a permanent basis by outsourcing as a result of globalization. In July 1981, many small consulting firms had begun to market their training programs to major corporations. Many companies were also looking to farm out their training needs and outsource them to outside firms. To reduce cost, training was a ripe area.

About that time, I was ready to leave Xerox. I had several offers, in addition to a Xerox offer for another assignment, but I decided to move on. I looked forward to taking Creative Investor Services in a new direction. What lay ahead were real estate syndications, private placement programs, and tax shelters.

Tips

Tip 1. *Research the company that will put you on the fast track.*
Review performance of your prospective company to determine that this is where you want to be. Studying the Xerox Corporation's operational data demonstrated that my new position placed me on a fast track.

Tip 2. *Stay focused on what's important.*
Showing discipline, focus, and the proper work ethic rather than becoming distracted will lead to more favorable results. A comment in the executive summary of the trip to Fort Lauderdale was that I kept focused on the job at hand and not recreation.

Tip 3. *Being an agent for change in a dynamic organization may put you aboard the fast track.* Implementing major changes in an organization and overcoming resistance is often associated with fast-track movements. Overhauling the entire training and development culture of the Xerox Corporation led to great benefits.

Tip 4. *Evaluations matter when aboard the fast track.*
On the fast track, decision makers determine how you are perceived and rewarded. A positive corporate audit of the new program provided for

invaluable support from senior management and acceptance of the changes within the company.

Tip 5. *In a fast-track environment, it helps to have a mentor or a role model.* Mentors and role models are often critical to survival and advancement in a fast-track company. Peter McColough, former Xerox CEO, provided invaluable insight and direction.

Summing Up

- Successful people look for the fast track to success. The plan you are following may not always deliver immediate benefits and gratification, but if you know that it is adding to your personal portfolio, stay with it.

- Be sensitive to your job environment in order that you can anticipate changes ahead that may affect your future. Awareness of your job culture will enable you to be prepared for change.

- Research the company that you are applying to and update your information once you are on the job. Researching your prospective job environment enables you to anticipate circumstances and know how best to deal with them.

- Successful people and successful corporations have a lot in common. They see challenges and not problems; they accept setbacks as temporary; and they live up to their performances because they expect it of themselves.

- Don't be caught short with inferior credentials if you know that they may limit you from taking advantage of the next opportunity. To be successful and to create wealth and independence, you must always go the extra mile by investing in yourself and staying on the fast track.

- Being an agent for change can be difficult but also rewarding. Being prepared and willing to be a change agent may lead to greater success.

- Evaluations do matter. Excellent performance leads to recognition that can result in major attitudinal changes by decision makers who determine the way you are perceived and rewarded.

- It helps to have a mentor. A mentor is often critical to survival and advancement, which is very helpful in a fast-growing and aggressive corporate environment.

Your Turn for Questions

- Are you on the fast track to success in your position? If not, what obstacles are preventing this?

- How might you navigate around these obstacles with the least effort?

- What opportunities have been presented recently in your career that you were unable to take advantage of? How could you have better prepared yourself for them?

- What resources are available in your current position that could help you make the most of unforeseen opportunities?

- If you were to look for a new job today, what prospects would you consider? How much do you know about those companies? How might you gather information about those companies to make you a more informed candidate?

- What opportunities do you have to affect change within your company? How might that change put you in better standing within your organization?

- How do you feel about your last performance evaluation? What could you do to improve the results of your next review?

- Do you have a mentor or role model within your organization? If so, how might you utilize their knowledge and experience to help you advance? If not, are there any candidates within your current circle of associates?

10

Focus on Wealth

Land is about the only thing that can't fly away.
Anthony Trollope (1815–1882),
English novelist

Most people confuse wealth and income, and they focus on income and not wealth. But the two are not the same. If you make a good income each year and spend it all, you are not gaining wealth. You are just living high. Income is what you take in; wealth is what you accumulate, not what you earn.

Many have been conditioned by their upbringing not to focus on wealth, but successful people and businesses *always* focus on it. Most people mistakenly believe that by concentrating on getting a larger income, they will automatically become wealthy. But it is much easier to get an increase in salary than it is to accumulate wealth. If you are increasing your salary but not increasing your wealth, you need to try another strategy. Being frugal with increasing income will do what increased income alone cannot.

Wealth is related to total net worth, having more than one form of income, and the capability of drawing upon large amounts of liquid assets or credit. It is seldom luck, inheritance, advanced degrees or even intelligence that makes it possible to amass wealth. Self-earned wealth is more often the result of a lifestyle of hard work, perseverance, planning, and most of all, self-discipline. You can't predict if someone is going to be wealthy by the type of business he's in. The character of the business owner is more important in predicting the level of wealth than the classification of the business.

Wealthy people are most often business owners, the self-employed, and entrepreneurs. Wealth builders invest a higher percentage of their income, apply their contributions to pensions and annuity programs, operate on a well-thought-out annual budget, and keep records of disbursements. Why are so few employees—often hard-working, well-educated, and with a fairly high income—wealthy? Earned income from a job is the slowest road to wealth creation. Earned income is taxed at a much higher rate than passive business income, leaving much less money to work with; and depending totally upon a paycheck doesn't encourage you to creatively develop plans to build wealth. Additional reasons could be the failure to pursue opportunities that exist in the marketplace, big spending, and not being price sensitive concerning consumer products and services.

There are certain common denominators among those who successfully build wealth. They choose what they are passionate about and determine how this passion can increase their wealth. They value financial independence. They are skilled in targeting market opportunities. They own appreciable assets. They live below their means, and they allocate their time, energy, and money efficiently in ways that are conducive to building wealth.

If you are seriously interested in creating wealth, leveraging real estate is one of the most critically important strategies you need to understand and employ. Leverage has overwhelming power because it is an investment strategy that uses other people's money or borrowed money.

There are several strategies to consider when selecting real estate locations for purchase. One of them is to seek out locations in growth areas with limitations on further growth. Urban properties will increase in value in limited geographical areas as raw land in the vicinity is used up. If you choose a first-class location, you will usually pay a premium for it; but it will almost always be worth it in the long haul.

Leveraging real estate has made many people very wealthy. More fortunes have been built in real estate than all the other fortune-building strategies, and wealthy people know the power of using leverage.

Experiences to Learn From

By delegating the day-to-day operations, Creative Investor Services continued throughout my tenure with Xerox. After leaving Xerox following my tenth year, I decided to add another product line to my business and started a real estate syndication company, Equity Properties, Ltd. As a securities broker-dealer and real estate developer, my company was ideally structured to purchase blocks of upscale Manhattan apartments not purchased by tenants during co-op conversions, and participate in securing investors for the syndication.

The premise was that Equity Properties would get a discount from what the price would have been if the apartments had been vacant. The discounts ranged up to about 50 percent of market value. If the tenant moved out quickly Equity Properties reaped a windfall, if not the company would hope to cover all or most of the costs with rents.

Investors who were prospects for purchasing an interest in the packaged apartments through Equity Properties would become subject to the New York City rent-stabilization laws regarding tenant rights. They would be responsible for supplementing any shortfall between the rents received from the rent-stabilized tenants and the co-op maintenance and other related expenses.

Since the syndication was being sold as a tax shelter as well as a long-term appreciating asset, investors secured by Equity Properties needed a legal opinion that the IRS would honor the specified terms of the tax shelter. I located a highly reputable Wall Street firm, Brown, Wood, Ivey, Mitchell & Petty, that agreed to do the legal work for me pro bono because their fees, added to the other fees, would kill the deal and because they were willing to use my syndication as a test case for this type of enterprise in a growth industry.

Next, I found a Connecticut bank that saw the growth potential of Manhattan real estate in the mid-1980s as relevant to their business plan, and was willing to supply the financing. I presented my syndication proposal to them. The timing must have been perfect, because after two meetings and completing the paperwork, I secured financing of more than $2 million, the entire financing for all of the apartments that I had initially selected. My new syndication company, Equity Properties, was off the drawing board.

The purchase agreements for the packages of apartments in several buildings were contingent upon my completing an offering memorandum and obtaining bank financing, which I had already arranged. Using other people's money (OPM) paid off.

When the market for tax sheltered real estate syndications dropped-off sharply with the new Tax Reform Act of 1986, I purchased apartments back from my investors who wanted to sell their interests and I carried the apartments for several years until they became vacant, free-market apartments. Those investors that held onto their purchased apartments from the syndication realized a great profit on their investment, as I did, when the market for Manhattan apartments appreciated geometrically. Using other people's money to invest in viable real estate is more often than not a lucrative investment tool and a wise wealth-creation strategy.

Tips

Tip 1. *Leveraging real estate is a great wealth creation tool.*
Use leverage for investing in real estate as a means of gaining the most by spending the least of your own money. I borrowed a hundred percent for my first spending deal when I launched my real estate syndication program.

Tip 2. *There may be opportunities with investment potential that are uncovered when delving into a new area.*
Showing initiative in new areas gives you added opportunities for building wealth. Expanding into residential real estate proved to be a lucrative venture.

Tip 3. *Prior to embarking on a new venture, research it thoroughly.*
Seek professional assistance when you are embarking on an unfamiliar venture. A major Wall Street law firm prepared the syndication documents.

Summing Up

- Most people confuse wealth and income. Wealth is what you accumulate, not what you earn.

- Most wealthy people are business owners, entrepreneurs, or self-employed.

- Earned income from a job is the slowest road to wealth creation.

- If you are seriously interested in creating wealth, leveraging real estate is one of the most critically important strategies you need to understand and employ.

- Showing initiative in new areas gives you added opportunities for building capital.

- When embarking on a new venture, do your homework and view it as an opportunity that you may want to consider.

- Be willing to seek professional assistance when you are embarking on something unfamiliar to you.

Your Turn for Questions

- How might you alter your life to begin living by the wealth-building strategies?

- Are you capable of developing and living within a budget?

- If you haven't created a budget yet, what has prevented you from doing so?

- Are you capable of cutting your consumption?

- Would you be willing to live beneath your means in order to build future wealth? If so, what could you do to reduce costs and live beneath your means?

- Do you own any appreciable assets? If not, what would be a possible asset to acquire, and what would it take to do that?

- What opportunities exist in your life to leverage other people's money?

- Is real estate in your area worth leveraging for profit?

11

Recognize Needs and Seize Opportunities

You don't get what you deserve, you get what you negotiate.
Chester L. Karrass (b.1923),
American negotiation expert and author

Your creative idea may be the door to opportunities that you are seeking. Recognize and take advantage of these opportunities, as they may not come around again. Successful people seize upon and capitalize on their creativity while others are reluctant to do so, either because of the belief that it is too difficult or they lack the knowledge as to how to proceed. One way to obtain the necessary knowledge to obtain a patent is through the U.S. Patent and Trademark Office in Washington DC.[3]

Your idea may be capable of yielding an income for you. If it is an invention, seeking a patent is a way to effectively test it. A patent for an invention is a grant of a property right by the government to the inventor (or his heirs or assigns) acting through the Patent and Trademark office ... What is granted is not the right to make, use or sell, but the right to exclude others from making, using, or selling the invention.[4]

There is no ceiling on the price to be paid for novel ideas. Behind every good idea is a wealth of knowledge. General knowledge is more abundant and more easily acquired than novel ideas. Because of this very truth, there is a universal demand and an ever-increasing opportunity for the person capable of generating sound novel ideas to sell them advantageously.

An unprotected idea is a lost idea, so take steps without delay to protect your novel idea through the patenting process. This should be done before sharing your idea with anyone, for two reasons. It sends a message to those to whom you disclose a concept that you are serious, and it helps to keep people honest.

If you are not ready or don't care to apply for a patent but want to officially evidence and register the conception date of your invention, the Patent and Trademark Office (PTO) offers a disclosure document program. For a nominal fee, the office will preserve your idea on file for a period of two years. This inexpensive recognition strengthens your case if any conflict arises as to the date of the conception of your idea. Send the Patent and Trademark office a paper disclosing the invention. Although there are no stipulations as to content and claims are not required, the benefits afforded by the Disclosure Document Program depend directly upon the adequacy of your disclosure. This is not meant as a replacement for the actual patent.[5]

The first step on the way to a patent is to conduct a search of all related inventions to see if what you are trying has been done before. The process of searching the voluminous archives is very structured. It is set up in a particular way so that it is relatively easy, although time-consuming, but anyone with determination and patience can do it. Once relevant classes and subclasses are identified, you need to obtain a list of all patent numbers granted for every class and subclass to be searched. This means that you have to search the complete text and drawings to find out how similar or different they were from your invention. All searches are available in Patent and Trademark Office designated public libraries.

While it is possible for a layman to successfully prepare and prosecute a patent application, the complexity of the laws, regulations, and formal requirements are often misunderstood or misinterpreted by those untrained and unfamiliar with the patent process. This leads to errors that are costly if not impossible to rectify.

To be granted a patent, the invention must be judged by the examiner to be unique, novel, and useful. The right granted by a patent is the right to exclude others from commercial exploitation of the invention; the person or company holding the patent is the only one who may make, use, or sell the invention. However, you may assign your rights in the invention to another person or company. The U.S. Patent Office recommends that all prospective applicants retain the services of a U.S. Patent Office registered patent attorney to prepare and prosecute their application. Patent attorneys are specialists and are consequently expensive. People occasionally confuse patents, copyrights, and trademarks, but they are distinctly different and serve different purposes.

An application filed in the Patent and Trademark Office and accepted as complete is assigned for examination to the respective examining groups having charge of the areas of technology related to the invention. In the examining group, applications are taken up for examination by the examiner in the order in which they have been filed.

The examination of the application consists of a study of the application for compliance with the legal requirements and a search through U.S. Patents, prior foreign patent documents and available literature, to see if the claimed invention is new and unobvious. A decision is reached by the examiner.

The applicant is notified in writing of the examiner's decision by an "action," which is normally mailed to the attorney or agent. The reasons for any adverse action or any objection or requirements are stated in the action, and such information or references are given as may be useful in aiding the applicant to judge the propriety of continuing the prosecution of the application.

If the invention cannot be patented, the claims will be rejected. If the examiner finds that the invention is not new, the claims will be rejected, but the claims may also be rejected if they differ only in an unobvious manner from what is found. It is not uncommon for some or all of the claims to be rejected on the first action by the examiner; relatively few applications are allowed as filed.

The applicant must request reconsideration in writing, and must distinctly and specifically point out the supposed errors in the examiner's action. After response by the applicant, the application will be reconsidered, and the applicant will be notified if claims are rejected ... The second Office action usually will be made final.[6]

Information in this chapter should not be relied upon as representing the Patent and Trademark's official information. All patent information should be obtained directly from the U.S. Patent and Trademark Office in Arlington, Virginia.

Experiences to Learn From

I had an idea and ended up with a patented product. It all began when my wife sustained a shoulder sprain in helping to dock our boat. She tried many different remedies for her pain, without much relief. The Jacuzzi with its pressure jet was the best, but it was only helpful when she was able to use it. I had the idea that I could fashion a portable device to simulate the effects of a Jacuzzi jet that she could use in our home shower whenever she wished. The portable pressurized water device could be applied to any area of the body that was in pain to get relief. My prototype was effective with her shoulder pain, and she was able to realize the effects of a Jacuzzi or whirlpool tub in the home shower every day without the unnecessary expense or time required.

Physicians have long recognized hydrotherapy, the use of water to enhance health, as increasing circulation and giving muscular pain relief. Hydrotherapy, a unique way to use nature's oldest medicine-water, benefits the entire body and can be used in a variety of ways without side effects to help control acute conditions. It became clear to me that hydrotherapy was a remarkable energizer that could also be used in first aid as well as to alleviate many other everyday problems. In restoring the energy flow, hydrotherapy helps the body to heal itself and prevents many other health problems from appearing. It is in the first line of health defense.

The first step on the way to a patent was for me to have a search of all related inventions to see if what I was trying to do was done before. I studied the results of the patent search carefully because you're out of luck if a previously patented invention is very similar to your idea, and your invention might even be infringing on another invention. On the other hand, one or more patents may describe inventions that are intended for the same purpose as yours, but are significantly different in various ways. Fortunately there were none of these, or I would have had to look those over and decide whether it was worthwhile to proceed. When my search showed that there was no similar invention, I immediately proceeded to the next step: to prepare to file a patent application.

My invention, and later the patented product, which I called *Hydro-Tone*, was designed to deliver pressurized water to any part of the body. The product did for my wife in the home shower what a whirlpool or Jacuzzi tub did, but it was portable and could be used as often as she wanted and as long as she liked, and it was possible to change the temperature of the water from hot to cold with ease, an important part of hydrotherapy. With my success, I entered the world of the inventor who needed to take an idea beyond the concept stage. This was the beginning of a very long journey.

As I looked through the patent rules and regulations, I did find them overwhelming. But I concluded that it was not cost-effective for me to engage a patent attorney at the start. So I headed down that complex road of the patent process on my own.

One bit of advice I received was, "Don't become emotionally attached to your invention." This is great advice, but it's hard to follow. It's like saying don't get attached to your children. I had started down this path, and I never wanted to give up on an idea or a challenge even after the arrival of my first office action citing deficiencies.

A friend referred me to Jim McKeever, a patent attorney from Greenwich, Connecticut, who was not actively practicing because he was confined to a wheelchair with multiple sclerosis. He became interested in my invention and decided to help me with the process after the return of a U.S. Patent Office action citing deficiencies. He understood the difficulty I faced in trying to navigate the patent process as a novice.

Jim reviewed the previous office actions received from the patent examiners to see how specific citations could be overcome. Jim had a file filled with all kinds of patent specialists that had experience with patent office specifications covering the field of mechanical drawing, engineering, prototype drawing, and prototype building.

On my visits with Jim, we talked about the patent process and the industry of inventing, and I learned a great deal from him. We developed a relationship beyond the invention and our talks became more than a client-attorney relationship as I visited with him during this terminal period. I revised the patent application with Jim's direction and decided that this time around I would try to arrange a meeting with my new examiner. I arranged an appointment and went to the Patent Office in Arlington, Virginia.

My assigned examiner was Danton D. DeMille. The name DeMille was unusual and familiar, and I asked him if he was related to the Hollywood mogul, Cecil B. DeMille. He told me Cecil was his uncle. He spent about an hour reviewing the technical points in the application and told me that it met the critical criteria—to be unique, novel, and useful—but the actual description of my claim in the document needed to be reworded. I incorporated his comments into my submission and, as he directed, restructured it in one paragraph of 199 words in a single sentence separated by semicolons and commas; the Patent Office requires this format so that all claims are uniform.

Several weeks after I submitted the reworded application, I heard from the examiner. He had a few additional questions that I answered, and within the next few weeks, I received the patent. The single claim that was fortunately accepted for my patent was very broad in scope, covering many aspects of a portable hydrotherapy device.

Jim, although very ill by this time and in a nursing home, advised me that once the utility patent was issued, I should follow up with a design patent, the second of two types of patents issued. A design patent is granted to someone who has submitted a new, original, and ornamental design for an article. The appearance of the article is protected by a design patent.

Jim referred me to a graphic designer, and I engaged him to do the mechanical designs. The design patent application was filed with the Patent Office, and several months later, I was granted a design patent. After years of hard work, trial and error, and persistence, I finally had a utility patent for my invention and a design patent for the design.

The entire process, from the first submission for the utility patent, to the patent office, the office action responses, the waiting period to resubmit, obtaining both the utility patent and the design patent, took a little over four years. I felt like celebrating when my patent arrived. It comes bound inside an oyster-white folder. The large, official gold seal of the Patent and Trademark Office is embossed upon it with two red ribbons furcated as a tail. Between the covers of this folder is your patent, a grant that gives you, the inventor, the right to exclude others from, making using or selling the invention throughout the United States and its territories and possessions for a period of twenty years (fourteen for a design patent) subject to the payment of maintenance fees as provided by law. I had produced the only portable hydrotherapy single-stream jet water shower massager.

Tips

Tip 1. *When a need arises, try to find a solution to the need.*
Ideas arise by seeking solutions to problems. By developing a pressurized therapeutic product, I was able to turn a personal need into a revenue stream.

Tip 2. *There is creative imaginative power in lots of ordinary people.*
Ordinary people can fully exercise their imagination and make it profitable. I'm not an engineer, nor would I consider myself a professional inventor. Nonetheless, I was able to structure my ideas into a useful and marketable product.

Summing Up

- Successful businesses develop a keen sense for recognizing and capitalizing on opportunities that may not come around again.

- Because unique ideas are not in abundance, there is a universal demand and an ever-increasing opportunity for a person capable of generating sound unique ideas to sell them advantageously.

- Because an unprotected idea is a lost idea, take steps to protect your unique idea through the patenting process. This should be done before sharing your idea with anyone.

- When a need arises, try to find a solution to the need. Ideas can arise from seeking solutions to problems.

- There is creative imaginative power in lots of ordinary people. Ordinary people can fully exercise their imaginations and make it profitable.

Your Turn for Questions

- Are you aware of any need in your life or in your social circle that could be fulfilled by a new or improved product?

- If so, what specific qualities would the product have?

- Why would it be novel?

- Are you aware of any novel modifications that could be made to an existing product in order to come up with a new and desired product?

- Who could you contact in your social circle to assist you with the creation and development process of a prototype?

- How do you think you would get started seeking a patent?

12

Handle Difficult People and Difficult Situations

> Put not your trust in money, but put your trust in trust.
> Dr. Oliver Wendel Homes (1809–1894),
> American writer and physician

Every so often, we must deal with difficult people and difficult situations, in spite of our best efforts. While most people are efficient, businesslike, and pleasant to deal with, and most problem situations can be resolved, there are times when difficult people and difficult situations persist. These unresolved situations can be obstructing, impeding and onerous.

The thing to remember when dealing with such occurrences is that it is highly unlikely that they are going to go away, and it is never easy or fun for anyone. However, to help with the process, know as much as you can about the persons or situations you are dealing with and this should give you valuable information and insight in handling it.

When you feel that negotiations are no longer working and the difficult condition persists, it could be time to bring in a fresh face. While this is not always practical, sometimes it is helpful to have someone who can negotiate for you. If that person reaches an impasse, you can resume as a new entity and perhaps change the situation, and, if this doesn't work and you are dealing in a business venture, it may be time to turn to an attorney. Lawsuits can be very expensive and stressful, and you need to know what you face before stepping into this arena. It is almost always better if the warring sides can reach a settlement before filing a legal case with the court. If a settlement cannot be negotiated, try to hire the best legal counsel you can afford.

When dealing with difficult people or situations, the tendency is some-times to procrastinate and put off bringing things to a head. For the busi-ness owner, delay in dealing with a difficult person or situation may make it increasingly costly. This is especially true if you are dealing with a sup-plier, partner, or a business deal. The actions that may have worked in the past, and is applied without regard for the new situation could end up with your not getting the desired outcome that you want. Unfortunately, many of us tend to use the same approach in all situations.

It is important when dealing with difficult people and situations to have a basic plan of action. Know what you intend to do before you launch into it. Think through what has to be done. Decide how you're going to do it. Review the plan with someone you can trust, and be candid with them. Make your plan realistic so that you can hold yourself to it, and be careful that you are not handicapped by the six major negative emotions: fear, jealousy, greed, hatred, revenge, and anger.

Businesses that employ a lawyer who is skilled in the area of the action at hand have fewer legal problems than those that do not. The dedication and competence of your lawyer is your best protection. The typical lawsuit begins when the plaintiff files a complaint with the court through an attor-ney. The plaintiff asks the court to issue a summons to the defendant noti-fying that person that a complaint is on file. The defendant then has a set period of time in which to file a response, which is an answer. The com-plaint, answer, and reply make up the pleadings of a case. The main pur-pose is to permit the court and the parties to identify the actual points at issue.

The complaint sets forth the plaintiff's version of the facts and a request for a certain remedy based on those facts. The defendant generally responds to the complaint by filing an answer or a motion to dismiss, usu-ally disagreeing with one or more allegations of fact set forth in the com-plaint. The answer also permits the defendant to raise legal points that will absolve the defendant of liability, even if his or her version of the facts is proven wrong.

Unless a controversy is settled by a judgment such as the granting of a motion to dismiss, or unless the parties settle out of court, a case will eventually come to trial. There, a jury will be impaneled, evidence presented, a verdict returned, and a judgment entered in favor of one of the parties.

Most people who suffer a variety of losses through the wrongdoing of others never seek redress of these grievances due to fear, mistrust of the justice system, or the cost of pursuing a legal case. With the proper knowledge and guidance, you can assess your situation yourself so that you can better evaluate your legal case *before* paying costly legal fees, and when you contact your attorney, you will be in a much better position to evaluate his advice. You may be better able to keep the management of your lawsuit and your legal costs under control and not suffer unnecessary financial loss, and hopefully you will end up with a financial gain or at least made whole.

Once you and your attorney explore the various possibilities of your grievance, and after contact with the opposition to ascertain whether an out-of-court settlement is possible, or, given the congestion of the state's court system, it may be possible to have your case heard before a dispute/resolution arbitration group. If not, your attorney may need to prepare to go to trial. Your attorney will then commence an action by serving the necessary papers on the other side. Many people will think that they can now sit back and relax and leave things in the hands of the attorney. But that would be a mistake. Your work has just begun. No one knows about the circumstances around your case better than you. Start to prepare yourself for the long, usually rough, road to the court.

Most cases go through an examination before trial (EBT) before they are argued before a judge or jury. It gives both sides the ability to size up their opponent's case. Be prepared to answer the issues placed before you by the opposing attorney in an EBT. Tell the truth, but only answer the questions that are asked.

One big problem facing the litigant is unexpected legal surprises, which often occur. There will be pretrial motions involving your case for which you may not need to be present. One pre-trial motion however, the summary judgment, is very important to you and you should try to attend because your entire case can be thrown out.

The most important step initially in the lawsuit is having the right lawyer. Competency among attorneys may have more to do with their style and faith in the case than with their talents. Which lawyer will fit the bill is a very hard call, and while you can always fire an attorney, finding a new one to take over the case is generally not easy. The best situation is to make sure that your attorney is a litigant. That means that your attorney has had a lot of experience in litigation and is comfortable with a jury.

What is written in this chapter is not intended to represent legal advice.

Experiences to Learn From

In one particular case, when I was in the manufacturing phase of my hydrotherapy invention, I engaged an intermediary, my engineer, to work on my behalf. I delegated to him direct contact with the manufacturing company that I selected to do the production work. This was done because they were both in the state of Maryland. However, that one decision created problems that could have been avoided had I taken the time out of my busy schedule to directly deal with the decision maker from the start.

My engineer assured me that he could act as my intermediary and work with the manufacturing company's engineer, his friend, to make sure that the molds from which the products were made would be of high quality, the production job was done correctly, and the timeframes spelled out in the contract were adhered to.

The contract required that all the molds would be completed by a specific date. The materials would have to be ordered, the color approved by me, the overmold for the ergonomical feature would be made to fit, and the nozzle and testing would begin after successful completion. I was delighted with the prospects that everything was spelled out in writing and seemed to be in place. Five thousand nozzles would be manufactured and ready for marketing according to schedule in time for sales for the holiday season.

In the meantime, I had to order the accessories—hoses, diverters, and thumb slides—to be fitted onto the final product. I contacted a company in Georgia that could supply the accessories and had them shipped directly to the manufacturing company so they would be available in assembling and packaging the product.

The manufacturing company failed to deliver the product as contracted. In fact, the product was not completed by the contracted date. It became apparent that the company had seemingly dragged its feet, and the owner of the manufacturing company wanted to renegotiate the entire contract. He wasn't happy with the money he was making.

He requested a change in the contract from a fixed price to a time-and-materials contract that would put him in control of the total cost for the manufacturing. When I reminded him that his signature was on the contract between my company and his, he said, "Well, you have the contract, but I have the molds and your accessories." It was clear that we were on a collision course. Overcoming this problem and securing my product required all of the skills needed to handle a difficult person and difficult situation.

Phone conversations with the owner over many months with promises to comply with the contract terms resulted in no change in the status quo. My engineer said he was completely dismayed by what was going on. It was clearly a stall to put pressure on me to allow the owner to change the terms of the contract. Things got worse when my engineer called me one afternoon to tell me that his friend had been fired by the owner and that the owner's son was now in charge of the production. With his friend out of the company, my engineer said he could no longer oversee what was going on. He was even further dismayed because he did not believe that the son had an engineering background that was necessary to manage the job or do the job. It was now clear that there would be no early resolution to this impasse. All production had now come to a halt. I sent a demand letter for the return of the accessories that had been shipped many months before to the manufacturing company for use in the assembly of the products. The owner refused.

Filing and pursuing a lawsuit against a company located away from your home state can be a major hurdle for any business. I was in Connecticut with no attorney licensed in Maryland. The manufacturing company was located where the lawsuit needed to be filed. My engineer said that he felt responsible because he had recommended the company largely because of his personal relationship with their engineer. What he didn't know at the time was that the owner had a reputation for using tactics and threats to evade the terms of contracts he signed. My engineer began to relate to me some of the history of the company that he was learning from his friend—information that would have been important to know before entering into the contract.

All was not lost, however, as part of his previously undisclosed history involved a breach of contract lawsuit filed against the manufacturer by another company. My engineer gave me the name of the law firm in Baltimore that a short time before had obtained a favorable settlement from the manufacturer because they did not want to go to court. I now had the name of a firm that might be interested in my case.

I called the firm, only to learn that the attorney who handled the case had retired. However, I was told to expect a call from another lawyer in the firm. I held my breath until I received the call. At first, the attorney from the Baltimore firm was not interested in the case. But after more discussion, he agreed to take the case for $3,000. He said I should send him a check immediately, which I did. Now, at least, I had an attorney that could represent me in the state of Maryland.

My attorney soon realized that this would not be a simple case to settle because of the manufacturer's cutthroat tactics. While many letters and phone calls went back and forth between the lawyers in an attempt to reach a settlement without going to trial, they were to no avail. My attorney decided to proceed to the trial stage, and we scheduled depositions.

When the company's attorney could not shake my testimony after deposing me for two days, he became visibly frustrated. My attorney asked him if we should break for a recess. It was clear that the tides had changed, and the company did not want to proceed to trial, as we were prepared to do.

It was then agreed in a settlement that the manufacturing company would turn over all of the molds and all of the accessories without any additional payment. The company could retain the deposit that they had received.

I examined a host of injection molding manufacturers, and following interviews with six companies I selected one from Leominister, Massachusetts, the current capital of injection molding. The selected manufacturer of invented product that now carried the name, HydroTone, produced thousands of quality products for marketing.

My *second* legal case came about following a closing of a group of co-op apartments that I purchased for syndication. *The New York Times* real estate section of Sunday, December 2, 1984, ran an article. It read:

The Market for Occupied Apartments is Expanding

"Winston E. Allen, founder of Creative Investor Services of Westport, Conn., a securities firm, is president of Equity Properties, Ltd., a syndication company that is buying occupied apartments mainly in groups … and re-offering them to small groups of investors. The investors hold an undivided interest in an aggregate number of shares in a particular building….

"The legal and filing fees are high, and this is not a deep tax shelter," Mr. Allen said.

The goal is long-term appreciation in value. This can be read in its entirety in the Appendix.

The board of one of the co-op buildings refused to transfer the shares into my name on the books and records of the co-op. I could not offer the syndication to investors until the proper documents were received and properly recorded. Only after my lawsuit was filed in October 1985, five months after the closing, did the co-op make the transfer of the shares into my name.

Real estate syndications were very competitive in the early 1980s because they provided a basis for a tax shelter; in other words, investments for higher-income investors. When the Tax Reform Act of 1986 changed the rules so that these deals could no longer provide that tax benefit, the refusal of the co-op to transfer the shares effectively put this syndication out of business. I could not move forward with the syndication in question because I would have had to disclose to prospective investors that I was unable to secure transfer of the shares because of the refusal of the co-op board to make the timely transfer to me and my company.

The question the court had to resolve in the lawsuit that I finally filed and won in a jury trial was whether the refusal to transfer the shares had been unreasonable, unlawful, and willful. Furthermore, if the refusal to transfer was illegal, did it result in my inability to sell, transfer, refinance the shares, sublet, or re-rent the apartments and cause my company irreparable injury?

The lawsuit was expensive, time-consuming, and diverted attention from other business matters. The case was tried by my attorney, Kevin Collins of Stamford, Connecticut, licensed to practice in both Connecticut and New York, but only after all attempts had failed to get a resolution.

After the verdict, one of the jurors, Joel F. Raven, senior vice president and managing director of the Capital Investment Group, as a juror was so moved by his experience that he wrote a letter and a lyrical poem and sent it to me as a testament to my tenacity and willpower. (It can be read in its entirety in the Appendix.):

March 12, 1990

Dear Mr. Allen:
As a plaintiff, you scored a direct knockout punch, so enjoy the attached. Just make sure it's pre-lunch. Best wishes for a continued success and best regards.

An opening statement
One more, then another,
It began to appear
That this case was a mother

The final arguments,
Closing, we learned;
Did the Allens just screw up?
Or did they get burned?

Sustained! Overruled!
That Same question's unneeded
I'll allow that! BE SEATED!

The third time around

And then lo and behold!
Don't believe that I heard it!
We took one more vote
And we got us a verdict!

The courtroom was hushed
Suspense too hard to bear
For the Allens it seemed
St. Nick soon would be there

On March 19, 1990, one week after the verdict, the *Connecticut Law Tribune* after an interview with my attorney, published the following:

Behind The Bar

Beginner's Luck? The fledging firm of Collins & Evans has yet to win a jury trial in Connecticut, but it's shown it can make it in the Big Apple. The firm won a $3.5 million verdict this month in a securities conversion case in New York State Supreme Court in Manhattan.

"This is the kind of thing you go through your life thinking it'll never happen and you luck into it," says Kevin F. Collins of the hefty award handed down March 8.

Collins, 32, who is licensed to practice in New York as well as Connecticut, formed the law firm with John J. Evans three years ago after each had served associate stints with local attorneys. Collins says he concentrates in personal injury law while Evans, also 32, focuses on commercial litigation. Although most of their business is in Connecticut, Collins says having the dual admission "has really helped us through the lean years. New York attorneys will give me work in Connecticut, and Connecticut attorneys will send me New York work," he says.

To bring home the $3.5 million verdict, the attorney represented Winston Allen, a Westport real estate developer and securities dealer, against the John Murray House Cooperative Association in Manhattan. Collins successfully proved that the association's board had failed to transfer ownership of the 14 percent stock in the co-op to Allen in a timely fashion, causing him to miss a significant business opportunity to resell the shares. Collins says he believes the fact that Allen is black at least partly motivated the board's delay in signing over the stock, which he borrowed approximately $2.2 million to purchase.

Allen says he turned to this firm because the firm had represented him in 1987 in a minor construction litigation matter and "did a very professional job." He also had recalled that Collins was admitted to practice in New York.

Collins says although he has had only one other jury trial—which he lost—since starting the firm, he expects more in Connecticut courts soon. "Our cases are going up the trial list, so it looks like we'll have more trials in the offing," he says.

But he wasn't so sure the firm would soon win another case of equal proportion. "It's not every day you win a three-and-a-half-million-dollar verdict," he laughs.

What isn't funny is that the firm did not take the case on a contingency basis—so Collins estimates the firm will earn only … based on its billable hours instead of the more than $1 million it should have netted under the typical 33 percent contingency arrangement. To the big dollars lost, Collins stoically replies, "It's a judgment call." Copyright© (1990) by Connecticut Law Tribune. Reprinted with permission.

The jury rendered a verdict in my favor and against the defendant. The court directed compensatory damages and punitive damages with interest paid to me. The verdict was appealed.

Tips

Tip 1. *When you have a product to manufacture, the most important single decision you make initially will be the selection of the manufacturing company.* The value of insisting upon quality will save you time and money. After my original manufacturer failed to deliver, I interviewed several manufacturers and my choice produced fine-quality products.

Tip 2. *Steer clear of negative people.*
Realize that people that are difficult can divert you, and hamper your chances of creating wealth. I set upon a plan that led to a positive outcome.

Tip 3. *Be astute when dealing with difficult people or situations, and have a step-by-step plan to obtain your objective.*
Don't become so frustrated with a difficult situation that you give up too early before finding a course of action. I was able to obtain the information from my engineer that was instrumental in obtaining a resolution of the difficulty.

Tip 4. *Do not hesitate to seek legal remedies in business when you know you have truly been wronged.*
Utilize competent legal services. When I missed a significant business opportunity, I became a plaintiff in a case against a co-op board.

Summing Up

- When you have a product to bring to market, a most important decision you make initially will be the selection of the manufacturer. The value of insisting upon contractual agreements being complied with can ultimately save you money.

- Realize that dealing with difficult people or difficult situations is never easy. For the business owner, delay in dealing with difficulties may cost you valuable time and money.

- Know who you're dealing with. The more you know about what motivates a person's behavior, the more you can avoid difficult people and situations.

- When involved in a civil lawsuit, you are subject to legal authority and face possible loss of capital and reputation.

- It is always better if the warring sides can reach a settlement before filing a legal case with the courts. If a settlement cannot be negotiated, hire the best legal counsel you can afford.

Your Turn for Questions

- What is the style and thinking characteristics of the person you are facing?

- What are your own thinking and negotiating styles?

- Are you likely to clash with the person you are facing?

- Can you adapt your style to gain the best outcome?

- Can you handle the situation if it is a tough one?

- Are you flexible enough to adapt to the needs of each situation?

- Are you tough enough to take the initiative when called for?

- Are you fact conscious when called for?

- Have you considered the considerable financial and emotional drain a lawsuit will cause? List all of those you can think of.

- If you had to proceed to court unexpectedly, do you currently have capable legal counsel? If not, what steps would you take to determine the qualities necessary?

13

Take a Risk and Bring Your Idea to the Marketplace

The second half of a man's life is made up of nothing but the habits
he has acquired during the first half.
Fyodor Dostoyevsky (1821–1881),
Russian novelist

A risk is taking a chance in which the outcome cannot be predicted and carries a probability of loss. Risk taking falls into many categories: career risks, relocation risks, and business risks, to cite a few. All risks are not equal, and some are just plain dumb. Learn to evaluate the risk you are considering, and if the investment of time and capital is small, it may be worth taking.

Dumb risks are pretty obvious and are recognized almost immediately. E-mails are filled with dumb risks, such as a person from a foreign country requesting that you put their money into your bank account but want you to show your honest intent by forwarding them money first. Hopefully, we all know to stay away from these risks.

However, it can be equally dumb to pass up risks with little investment but where the potential downside is very limited and can be rewarding. We need to learn more about taking intelligent risks and begin to make changes in how we think of ourselves as risk takers and to what extent we can afford the risks we are considering.

People who take risks tend to be the achievers in our society. They are long-range thinkers who look ahead to possible long-term payoffs. They are often not content with the status quo. To them, they see risk taking as the doorway to success, and for them, the higher the risk, the more exciting the venture. This group of risk takers is in the small minority.

Developing your ability to handle risks is a lifelong process. The smart thing to do is begin with low-risk situations and gradually increase your confidence level, enabling you to become comfortable as the risks increase. Consider giving up your leisure time and paying for an educational or training program that could lead to your opening up a business. If the venture does not pan out, you still retain the knowledge you gained, and it may become useful to you later. A low-risk business for you may be an online business venture, which may simply involve a computer, a modem, and a line into your own home. Find an intelligent risk you can take. Celebrate whether it pans out or not, because no matter what the outcome, you'll gain courage just by making the attempt, and you will have learned something.

New ventures are inherently risky because there is no guaranteed outcome, and the possibility of not being successful is always present. Manufacturing a new product is not without considerable risk, and many people who have a worthy product or service idea do not try to go further because they don't believe they can be successful. The possibility of failure, however, need not stop you if you believe in what you are seeking to do, provided you are willing to persevere and work hard.

But once you've taken that initial risk and brought an idea to fruition, marketing it is your next big challenge. Every type of entrepreneurial venture requires marketing to be successful. One factor that determines success or failure is the way you introduce your product. Business owners who are involved in launching a new product or service need their name or their company's name out in public, competing with other companies that are trying to do a similar thing.

Entrepreneurial marketing is very different from conglomerate marketing. An entrepreneur must have a different outlook in order to survive and must apply different principles than the president of a large or midsized corporation. An entrepreneur is usually not a widely diversified corporation, but an individual profit making business. To prosper, he must use different tools such as, new on-line technology software that evolved during the last twenty years that delivers smart commerce solutions, order management and customer services as marketing has become less of an art and more of a science. A large company can invest in an expansive advertising campaign run by an ad agency, and that company if not successful, can hire a different agency the second time around. This luxury is not usually available to entrepreneurs, who need to be right the first time. They don't have the level of resources of large corporations that can change their advertising strategies whenever it is necessary.

Individual entrepreneurs can flourish by gaining a tiny slice or fraction of a market. You also need a better presentation and a focused strategy. It is not enough to have a better idea. All of your marketing must be pulling in one direction. The core idea must extend to the company brochures, the Web page, the Yellow Pages advertising, and the direct mailing. Marketing is largely a product of opportunity, timing, and funding. All marketing methods can be successful, but it generally requires a large investment of capital.

Marketing and selling are often confused. Marketing involves bringing the customer to the product, while sales involves bringing the product to the customer. Both strategies are useful. The route you decide upon will be clearer if you can state the main concept in fewer than eight words. Your marketing plan requires that you attend to all details, engage in research, and know your targeted audience. A product benefits when it differs from its competition and is difficult to copy.

If you are comfortable with your responses to these issues, then you may have a new idea that is worth pursuing. Patience is an important attribute when you launch a new marketing plan. If you expect instant results, your plan will never have a chance to gain a foothold or have an impact on the marketplace. Give your marketing plan time to take hold. If you have carefully thought it through, have confidence in your plan, and put your plan into action, it could pay rich dividends. Stick with it. By having an appreciation for the importance of marketing and following the ideas in the introduction to this chapter, you have an increased chance of becoming successful in your new venture.

Experiences to Learn From

To share my invention with others, I had to turn my idea into a tangible form. Then I went on the road to put the ideas into practice. I was about to embrace the world of design, prototypes, and mold-making. I needed to learn quickly about the entire process and have the services of an engineer to build the prototype. I also needed to learn about mold machinery, injection molding, and a host of other processes. I also made the decision that the product would be manufactured in the United States.

I first market-tested my HydroTone by going into the field and having people try the product and respond to questions about it. Once it was received well, I presented it at trade shows, TV shopping networks, and in catalogs. I created a Web site to do Internet marketing under the Web address www.innovativehydrotone.com. My hydrotherapeutic product with its 40 to 85 pounds per square inch (ppi) was a new idea and therefore did not have head-to-head competition.

Getting prospective customers to use and receive the benefits of a product is a time-honored sales technique. The importance of a proper and complete product demonstration can hardly be overemphasized. I had a large portable transparent enclosure built to demonstrate the model that I took to trade shows that showed the powerful single-stream hydrotherapy effect. My demonstration model attracted prospects who placed their hands and arms into the Plexiglas case and experienced the stimulating effects of the therapeutic water pressure and its treatment use in reflexology. Some of the best results came from marketing HydroTone at trade shows and home shopping networks because prospective end users and distributors could see firsthand how this simple-to-install and use product produced remarkable results.

Tips

Tip 1. *The goal of marketing is to successfully introduce a product or service.* Having various methods for exposing your product or service can be profitable. I introduced HydroTone at trade shows, and catalogs.

Tip 2. *Brand name or name recognition is important.*
Get your brand name in the public domain for the greatest success. Through persistence, and hard work I was able to gain national exposure on a television shopping network and on the Web site.

Tip 3. *Marketing is largely a product of creativity, money, and opportunity.*
Even with a limited budget, research unique ways to get your product known. I promoted HydroTone for eight minutes on a shopping network with good results.

Summing Up

- In your business ventures, start by taking acceptable risks and gradually increase your confidence level, enabling you to become comfortable as the risks increase. Working with a new venture is inherently risky because there is no guaranteed outcome and the possibility of not being successful is always present.

- To be successful when introducing a new product as an entrepreneur, you must become a master at marketing. Give your marketing plan time to take hold.

- Marketing is a complex process and can be the most difficult and expensive in achieving success. Marketing includes everything that you do to promote your product or service.

- The goal of marketing is to successfully introduce a product or service. Having various methods for exposing your product or service can be profitable.

- Marketing is largely a product of opportunity, creativity, and money. Even with a limited budget, research interesting ways to get your product known.

Your Turn for Questions

- What might an important step be in promoting your product or idea?

- How do you think your endeavor might be creatively or specifically marketed?

- Who do you think the target audience would be?

- What are the appropriate venues for marketing and promoting your product?

- What are some inexpensive or free methods of marketing your product?

- How will this information be incorporated into your developing business plan?

14

Increase Your Knowledge of Money

There is nothing about money that cannot be understood by the
person of reasonable curiosity, diligence and intelligence.
John Kenneth Galbraith (1908–2006),
economist

General knowledge about money is a critical gap in our educational system, as there is almost no one teaching it. The academics have too little
practical experience, and the rich keep their secrets. Acquiring knowledge
about money is not a casual undertaking; it needs to be a planned
endeavor. Most people have to teach themselves about money through
trial and error, often with a costly and lengthy learning curve. You can
start your money education by defining your spending goals, listing your
regular expenses, and creating a cash reserve. You also need to know how
to maintain a budget, make a habit of shopping wholesale, live within your
means, perfect your credit, know how to invest your money smartly, don't
spend what you don't have, and make your house a financial asset.

Taking a page out of the strategies used by wealth builders—those
whose profession is making money for themselves and others—can help
you assemble what information and knowledge about money is absolutely
essential. Wealth builders have a keen understanding about money—the
way they think about money and the way they use money. Wealth builders
are knowledgeable in the areas of real estate, securities, taxes, and accounting. Successful wealth builders recognize when their knowledge base will
directly affect their ability to generate income and pursue education
accordingly.

Your predominate amount of self-education, studying, and reading should take place during your money-earning productive years. If a lack of knowledge about any or all of the basic money areas is your problem, you need to work on acquiring the knowledge you lack.

Courses on real estate development, tax deductions, and budget plans are some of the ways to start your financial education. To some, these programs are boring, but when you develop the habit of studying to improve your money knowledge, you will likely continue for the rest of your life. Once you undertake a program about money and planning for your financial success, your wealth building is underway.

Many people do not know much about the wealth they have, which makes it difficult for them to manage effectively their personal financial affairs. This applies even to sophisticated people who have reason to know something about managing their money. Some top executives who handle their companies' monies are failures at managing their own. As it turns out, once they understand their deficiencies, many are able to teach themselves what they need to know and how to handle their money on their own. Financial sophistication comes through developing an investment mentality and learning and practicing the rules of the game. In short, you need to perfect your ability to handle money.

If you've never calculated your net worth, you may be in for a surprise—maybe even a pleasant one. No single step in increasing *your* money IQ is more important than the annual calculation of your net worth. To determine your net worth, add up the value of everything you own, such as stocks, bonds, real estate, the current value of your business, if you own one, the value of your residence, if you own one, and then subtract everything you owe. Net worth is the measure of your wealth, because, if necessary, what you own can be eventually liquidated into cash and is the financial value of everything you own. This is your scorecard in the game of wealth building. The growth of your net worth is the measure of your success. Since your main goal is achieving financial independence, you can measure your success with the annual computation of your net worth.

Being knowledgeable about money pursuant to becoming financially independent provides you with the mindset to pursue interests and passions that transcend self and have a positive influence on the lives of others. All philanthropists recognize the many needs in their communities and beyond, and are willing to contribute to making a difference in the lives of others. Giving something back provides an opportunity to express appreciation for all that you have achieved. Building a rich legacy of giving can become a necessary part of your plan. With your contributions and influence, you can shape the lives of young people and even future generations.

You are now on the way to recognizing why some people acquire great amounts of money and self-fulfillment and others do not. In fact, you can be one of those people who do.

Experiences to Learn From

A firsthand account of the techniques I used to insure my financial knowledge and security is recapped here. My career spanned forty-five years, in which time I managed multiple overlapping interests. No matter how much I knew as a professional, I realized I could not rely upon yesterday's knowledge when dealing with money, investments, and estates today. I learned early that there are no free lunches, and the guidance I provide in this book cannot be had without a price, although the price of what you have to expend on your own is far less than the value that will accrue to you.

As an NASD broker-dealer, financial planner, and real estate developer, I have conducted financial workshops on investing, trading, financial planning, and money management. I learned early that the best way to master a subject is to teach it to someone. This was again clear to me when I trained sales reps for the NASD exam and taught them the principles of money, investments, and other finance areas that they were not familiar with. I grounded them in these subjects to enable them to handle various finance-based investment opportunities for their clients and for themselves.

Conferring with financial institutional investment companies provided a continuous opportunity to upgrade my knowledge, the knowledge of my sales reps and my clients. Researching investment companies' prospectuses and preparing my own prospectus for distribution also expanded my capacity to pass along my money knowledge to others.

Knowledge is one of the most important factors for clients to utilize when purchasing investment products. When I structured real estate syndications and organized and promoted the new entities, I expanded the knowledge of my prospects and coupled it with knowledge of real estate values, locations, and risks, which they needed to be sophisticated practitioners. The knowledge I provided enabled them to examine the profit opportunities of the properties and understand the risk-benefit ratio. Another aspect of money knowledge is estate planning that I imparted, an area that most people avoid educating themselves about because it deals with their own mortality.

In addition to the knowledge I have attempted to pass on to others about money, finances, entrepreneurship, and financial independence, the lasting lesson I learned was that entrepreneurship is ongoing. As great as the ten years were that I spent at Xerox Corporation and the knowledge and rewards that I received from working in top management of an American company, when it's over, it's over. When you work for yourself, it's never over. I am grateful for the opportunity I had to start and build my own businesses from the bottom up: Creative Investor Services is still operational today, the real estate syndication business provides me with residuals and property ownership, and my company is marketing my invention. The point I wish to make is that when you create something like a business, a product or a concept, unlike a job, it can be yours forever.

Tips

Tip 1. *Knowledge of handling money is a key to wealth creation.*
Learning about money is an essential step in wealth building. Acquiring knowledge of money and its handling was essential to my business. Building on that knowledge is still an ongoing process.

Tip 2. *Protect your assets.*
Estate planning is an important part of your money IQ. I used the principles and practices of estate planning to secure assets and plan for the future.

Tip 3. *Self-education should take place during your money-earning productive years.*
Constant learning about your field is essential. I take graduate and continuing-education courses periodically.

Tip 4. *Annually calculating your net worth is a very important step in your money IQ.*
Knowledge of your net worth is your scorecard in the game of wealth building.
I calculate my net worth annually for record keeping and information purposes.

Summing Up

- Knowledge about money is a critical gap in our educational system.

- Money and finance are governed by the equivalent of scientific principles. Readers who choose to follow the simple rules and strategies of financial independence and wealth building can realize a rich, rewarding, and satisfying life. Those who don't may end up frustrated and angry.

- Although the amount of money required for financial independence differs from person to person, financial independence is the realization of financial objectives on a preplanned basis.

- Accumulating wealth and knowledge about money is not a casual undertaking; it should be a planned endeavor.

- Having knowledge of money provides you with the mental set to pursue interests and passions that transcend self and have a positive influence on the lives of others.

- Accumulating wealth is something you need to plan, so beef-up your understanding of handling money.

- Few ordinary citizens know much about the wealth they have, which makes it difficult for them to effectively manage their personal financial affairs. This applies even to intelligent and sophisticated people who have reason to know something about managing their money.

- Knowledge of handling money is a key to wealth creation. Learning about money is an essential step in wealth building.

- Protect your assets. Estate planning is an important part of your money IQ.

Your Turn for Questions

- From where has your existing education about money and finance come?

- Do you feel that you have a sufficient education about money and finance?

- What steps could you take to decrease your knowledge gap and increase your knowledge about money?

- How might you start early to begin investing income?

- How might you operate your household with a budget?

- How might you plan consumption?

- How might you sacrifice high consumption today for financial independence tomorrow?

- Are you currently engaged in a financial plan? If not, what three steps could you take today to begin a financial plan?

- Do you currently give back to the community? If not, what do you think could be gained by doing so? And what's stopping you?

- What do you hope your future legacy will be? What are you doing today to ensure that?

- How many of the above steps to financial independence do you currently practice? What would it take to implement all nine steps into your life?

- Have you incorporated any facets of estate planning into your current financial plan?

Afterword

We all experience a vision of what we desire to become; we envision an image of our future. A vision helps determine the ideal to which you are striving. Now that you know the wealth-creation formula, what are your dreams, hopes, and vision for your future? Before answering this question, it is important to note that having wealth and being rich is measured in terms that far exceed money. It is not simply the acquisition and ownership of resources and property and self-fulfillment. It comes with great responsibility too.

I've identified principles and illustrated methods for avoiding the pain of financial and emotional distress caused by being unprepared. These methods are unique. They are not gender, age, or race specific. I've shown how my methods can be applied and how they work. I've given you an antidote to overcoming fear, while at the same time providing motivation and inspiration to fill a void during unsettling and disruptive times.

The guidance I received in my education and experience cannot be purchased with money. The advice given to me cannot be purchased at any price by those who are not intentionally searching for it. It serves only those who are ready for it, and you should have the answers before you finish this book. You may find your answers in the very first chapter or on the last page. This could be a turning point in your life. Somewhere as you read this book, the guide to which I refer will jump from the page and stand boldly before you. If you are ready, you will recognize it when it appears. Remember, too, this book deals with facts and not with fiction. I want to convey a great universal truth through which all who are ready may learn what to do and how to do it. If you haven't already, you will also receive the needed stimulus to make a start. The key is that all achievement, all earned riches, have their beginning with an idea.

Endnotes

1. Congressional Budget Office, Baby Boomers in Retirement: An Early Perspective (Washington, DC. September, 1993); xi.

2. Rand Corporation (Santa Monica, California) n.d., n.p.

3. U.S. Department of Commerce, Patent & Trademark Office, General Information Concerning Patents (Washington, DC, 1990); 1–5.

4. Ibid—20–21

5. Ibid.

6. Ibid—22–23

Appendix

The Westchester Business Journal
November 4, 1969

Winston E. Allen: Combines Careers To Build Multi-Service Investment Firm

By Peter Singer

When an educator in the field of economics decides to put his theories into practice, chances are he'll do more than make his mark in the business world.

Fulbright scholar, college professor, and investment counselor Winston E. Allen of Larchmont is founder and head of Creative Investor Services, Inc., a multi-service investment firm based in New York City. Mr. Allen has recently announced the opening of Creative Investor's Westchester Division, located in the Pershing Square building in New Rochelle.

"A primary purpose of this new division," Mr. Allen noted, "will be to bring to the Westchester black community unusual investment and career opportunities. Professionally trained blacks are unfortunately conspicuous by their absence in the world of Wall Street."

Finding Personnel

Mr. Allen is uniquely qualified to remedy this situation. His career as an educator (he taught economics at DeWitt Clinton High School, a course for teachers at City College's Graduate School of Education, and directed the college discovery program at one of the city universities) has enabled him to surmount his biggest hurdle, finding personnel. Since Mr. Allen found that there "were very few black registered representatives working in the nation's brokerage houses," he decided to develop and train his own staff, a move that would help additional people gain a foothold in the securities business.

"The Westchester division will be a center of recruitment and training, as well as a center for providing an investment service to local residents, both black and white."

Mr. Allen emphasized that his firm is fully integrated. "Right now in New Rochelle, we have 15 people in training, black and white, men and women. Most of them have teaching or civil service backgrounds. Our customers are integrated as well. We want to provide an investment service for all Westchester residents. We demonstrate the ways a second income can be developed for individuals who invest their surplus dollars into our company's creative capital plans. Since the test given prospective securities personnel by the National Association of Securities Dealers is a difficult one, we start our people from scratch and teach them the fundamentals. When they finish a one month crash course and pass the N.A.S.D. exam they become part-time salesmen until they become established; then they become full-time producers."

Mr. Allen noted that his graduates are paid "very high commissions," and none has yet been lured away by other businesses. His staff of 43 salesmen accounted for more than $2 million in ... sales this year. Creative Investors is affiliated with the Detroit Stock Exchange.

Mr. Allen [has] managed a dual career since 1958, as an educator and a registered representative involved in the securities field. "One career strengthened the other, for example, the evaluation I did for the job core [Job Core] under the auspices of the Office of Economic Opportunity, showed me how many people were working in dead end jobs which in turn gave weight to my ideas for Creative Investors. Theory and practice did strengthen each other. I founded Creative Investors in 1962, and when it began to demand more and more of my time, I decided to make a full commitment to the firm in 1968."

New careers are nothing new to Mr. Allen. His interest as a high school student was music. A native of New York City, he graduated from the prestigious High School of Music and Art where he studied music, the piano specifically. After a BA from New York University, he received a Masters degree and was awarded a Fulbright grant at the Institute of Political Studies in Paris. He is a candidate for his doctorate at Fordham University.

"Outside interests? I dearly love to travel. Ever since my Fulbright days in Paris, I've managed to get back to Europe six or seven times and to the Middle East and Africa as well. I enjoy music, and I play the piano ... I don't have much free time these days ... Mr. Allen's projections for Creative Investors include "expansion of [the] divisional office. We're interested in developing a broad base of operations in the investment field. We have plans for that sort of development. Eventually we hope to expand the underwriting business and to use the broker-dealer license to trade stocks. I think perhaps we're tapping a market that is ready for a piece of the action."

Finance

The Magazine of Money
December 1969

Up Allen's Alley

Many minorities lack economic power. One solution to their problem lies in education. Winston Allen, the 36-year-old founder and head of the black-owned and run Creative Investor Services, is well aware of this and is trying to whittle away at the educational gap between Wall Street and blacks.

First, he had to dispel the myth that business couldn't be done in black communities. So in 1962, running a one-man show, he sold $1 million in … funds. "The money was there, especially in the case of civil service workers, but lack of knowledge about investments had bred distrust," says the articulate executive. "I used personal contact. Besides, I was selling … funds with proved records."

Now that he has a staff, Allen uses seminars to acquaint the people with the benefits of investing. He says the turnout is good.

His next problem was recruiting sellers. Most had some college education, but none had any appreciable experience in the brokerage business.

So Allen, a former teacher at City College, set up a home training program. "We now run a four-week crash course with Saturday classes and a mountain of homework," he says. More than 35 of the students have passed the stringent NASD test for selling equities and become versed in the world of finance. As a result, Creative now offers other services, such as insurance.

But the soft-spoken yet aggressive Allen won't stop there. He says, "There are plenty of black entrepreneurs who don't have proper capitalization but who do have good business ideas. The field is virtually untapped." He believes small syndicates can be formed to finance these potentially profitable businesses.

Allen plans to expand to many other cities but wants to avoid the pitfalls of expanding too quickly. Certainly, more than 90 percent of his clients live in black communities, but he thinks integration of the firm will broaden its base and help in the long run.

Helping people make money while making it yourself is a happy but somewhat risky undertaking. Like most creative people, Allen makes it look easy.

Finance magazine's article Magazine of Money, the December 1969 issue, featured *People in Finance*, which profiled *Winston Allen, CEO of Creative Investor Services*, along with other high performers in the field. Individuals such as Andrew J. Melton, incoming president of the Investment Bankers' Association and chairman of Smith, Barney & Co.; I. W. Burnham, founder of Burnham & Co., an investment banking house; Leonard Rose, president of the National Account Systems, the largest collection service chain in the world; and W. W. Keen Butcher, managing partner of Butcher & Sherrerd, Philadelphia Investment banking firm were featured. Copyright © (1969) Finance. Reprinted with permission.

The New York Times
Wednesday, July 31, 1968

Crash Course Creates Salesmen:

By Robert D. Hershey, Jr.

"We try to find people who are working in dead-end jobs. Then we put them through a one-month crash course so they can pass the NASD exam."

This is the way Winston E. Allen is acting to expand the sales force of Creative Investor Services Inc., an investment concern he founded in 1962.

The company, based at 550 Fifth Avenue, is involved mainly in selling securities. In an interview the other day, Mr. Allen said he expected that his dozen salesmen would account for $1 million in fund sales this year.

Finding men is probably Mr. Allen's biggest problem. It has been estimated that there are only 60 black registered representatives working in the nation's brokerage houses, a small reservoir from which to draw if he had decided to try to hire them away.

A better idea, he thought, would be to develop his own personnel, a move that would help additional blacks to gain a foothold in the securities business.

"Training is the chief bottleneck," he declared, noting that the test given to prospective securities personnel by the National Association of Securities Dealers was "difficult." particularly for those with little familiarity with the business.

The best way to handle this is to get them licensed to sell some sort of securities. "We start from scratch and teach them the fundamentals," Mr. Allen said.

The head of Creative Investor Services (Mr. Allen calls himself executive director) does much of the training himself, but recently he has enlisted the help of the Presidential Life Insurance Company, a young concern situated in Nyack.

Presumably, the salesmen will soon be selling insurance as well as fund shares.

Mr. Allen, who is active in many self-help civic programs, has taught economics at DeWitt Clinton High School and at Queensborough Community College. This summer he is teaching a course for the teachers at the City College Graduate School of Education, designed to help them work with the children of the poor.

About 20 men are now taking the crash course, on which they spend about 15 to 20 hours a week. Many of the sessions are held at Mr. Allen's home in Larchmont.

When they finish and pass the exam, they will become part-time salesmen until they become established. Then, it is hoped, they will become full-time producers.

Mr. Allen said his "graduates" are paid very high commissions and none has yet been hired away by other businesses. "These men are becoming very attractive," he declared.

Eventually, Mr. Allen plans to expand the underwriting business of Creative Investor Services and to use its broker-dealer license to trade stocks. Demand for investments, Mr. Allen says, has been "overwhelming."

The company participated in the spectacularly successful distribution of Gerald Tsai Jr.'s Manhattan Fund, Inc. when it was offered publicly in 1966.

Creative Investor Services is affiliated with the Detroit Stock exchange.

Xerox World
June 1973

The Center in Leesburg

On June 2, 1973, The Xerox International Center for Training and Management Development opened its doors to its first students—Xerox sales and service people.

The Leesburg Center is the culmination of a Xerox dream to offer the best training and development programs to its people.

When the center is in high gear, technical representatives, sales representatives, computer scientists, managers—and more than a thousand students at a time—will be educated in its elaborate facilities on a 2,265-acre site in rural Leesburg, Virginia.

This special section of *Xerox World* is devoted to the Leesburg Center—its history, its philosophy, its realty, and its future.

Leesburg: A Xerox Commitment to the Development of its People

By Mandi Harris

Research in Education

"Xerox has always had a commitment to people development," said Dr. Winston Allen. "This center is the ultimate. Here we have the opportunity to be the pioneers in industrial training."

And if Xerox is the pioneer, Allen could be called the wagon master. He is the Leesburg Center's manager of education research and development. This department works side by side with the Rochester curriculum group and the Center's school managers. They decided what is to be taught, and Allen's group works out with them the best way to teach it.

Allen and his staff are in-house experts on how people learn. They bring to the Center the latest know-how in behavioral science, research, curriculum, and instructional technology. They determine the best method of instructing for particular courses, and provide structure for the training programs. "In other words," said Allen, "we define the best way to get the message across."

Very often, that method is visual. It has been found that people learn best through seeing and doing. So, interaction plays an important part in the Center's training programs. The idea is to make the classroom experience as close to real life as possible.

"That's why there is a lot of importance placed on the role-playing technique," Allen said. These role-plays are videotapes and replayed by the students; they learn by watching themselves and correcting their mistakes.

"We have used videotaping in the previous training schools," Allen said, "but not to the degree that it is used here at Leesburg."

"The octagon-shaped classroom is another innovation in education strategy," Allen said. It is based on the concept of give-and-take between the instructor and student, and between student and student.

"They learn from each other as well as from the instructor," he said. "The lecture process isn't as effective largely because the students play a very passive role. In our program, they're very active. The more active the students are, the more they learn."

The very idea of a Leesburg Center—in which students from all over the country come to one place to pursue several disciplines—extends beyond the classroom by giving students a chance to see what is on the other side of the fence, to learn to appreciate business disciplines other than their own.

"Through this interaction," said Allen, "the students become better aware of the direction of the company, which in turn fosters professional growth and development.

"Here we can test new teaching methods, new media, and new techniques for introducing multimedia into the curriculum. We can further develop and implement our own research design to further enhance our training products. This Center is second to none in capabilities and potential."

In its short existence, the Center has already been visited by interest groups ranging from Army Training Specialists to Harvard University professors. "It's entirely possible," said Allen, "that instructional techniques developed at Leesburg will eventually be adopted by traditional learning institutions."

"And we're working closely with several colleges and universities," he said, "with an eye toward developing accredited program here for our own people—courses in business administration, educational technology and psychology." Copyright © (1973) by Xerox World. Reprinted with permission.

The New York Times
Real Estate

Sunday, December 2, 1984

The Market for Occupied Apartments is Expanding
Blocks Purchased for Resale Attract More Investors

By Alan S. Oser

Investors in Texas find it hard to understand the prices of apartments in New York City.

"They can't comprehend paying $30,000 a room," says Gary H. Herman, an officer of D. G. B. Property Corporation, a real-estate syndicator that has bought several rental buildings in Manhattan," when in Texas you could pay $25,000 for an entire apartment with two bedrooms and two baths.

Accordingly, buyers from around the country have not generally followed the approach of this New York—based syndicate—buying rental buildings at prices that reflect not their present or prospective value after conversion to condominiums or cooperative. At that point, the product available for investment is not only vacant apartments, but increasingly, as conversions take the noneviction route, the occupied apartment renters decline to buy at insider prices.

Not all sponsors put these renter-occupied apartments up for sale. But others, once accumulated vacancies are sold and insider buying has subsided, are ready to sell the remaining renter-occupied units to outside investors at varying discount-from the value as a vacancy, at which point the apartment is normally resold for occupancy.

Sales of these renter-occupied apartments in some cases are being promoted aggressively. An example is the Hanover companies' attempted through Ahrens Barrell of occupied apartments in developments such as Parc Vendor in Manhattan and Glen Oaks in Queens. Cumulatively, the company reports sales of 1,800 apartments to outsiders, with buyers taking only a single apartment in almost all cases.

Other sponsors sell mainly through private placements of blocks of shares representing several apartments. The buyers are high-income individuals with no interest in living in the apartments but who expect eventually to gain in a resale of a vacant apartment while benefiting from tax shelter during the holding period. Recently, this "aftermarket" has been joined by packagers who are reselling to other individuals or investment groups.

Stimulating the market has been the growing availability of financing. Most importantly, the Federal National Mortgage Association, known as Fannie Mae has begun to buy such loans from prime lenders, thus creating greater lender willingness to supply the financing. And Citibank has developed a pilot program to test the market for renter-occupied apartments, designed mainly for buildings in which Citibank has provided the primary financing.

In all cases, the premise is that the buyer gets a discount from what the price would be if the apartment were vacant. The discount can range up to 50 percent of market value. If the tenant moves out quickly, the buyer can reap a windfall. If not, the buyer hopes to cover all or most of his cost with rent. The tax benefits of depreciation and interest and property-tax deductions will make up much of any deficit for some time.

Under the Citibank pilot program, the bank will lend up to 90 percent of an amount that cannot exceed 65 percent of the apartment's value if vacant, as determined in a bank appraisal. Thus, if the apartment has a market value of $100,000 Citibank will provide up to 90 percent financing on a purchase price up to $65,000.

Sponsors themselves have typically been the major suppliers of financing for individual buyers of occupied apartments thus far.

The bulk buyers of occupied apartments are occasionally groups planning to resell to individual investors. For example, Mary Sue Morris, a real estate broker and developer said she had bought 25 apartments in two buildings in partnership with Peter Frank of Los Angeles and was planning to buy 50 more. The resales are private placements of packages of two apartments, priced at a 40 to 45 percent discount from vacancy value, she said. The buyers are investors with a net worth of at least $1 million.

"I only buy apartments in pre-World War II buildings, with big windows and rooms-the kind of apartments I know I could sell and would want to live in myself," she said.

Winston E. Allen, founder of Creative Investor Services of Westport, Conn., a securities firm, is president of Equitable Securities, Ltd., a syndication company that is buying occupied apartments mainly in groups ... and reoffering them to small groups of investors. The investors held an undivided interest is an aggregated number of shares in a particular building.

"The legal and filing fees are high, and this is not a deep tax shelter" Mr. Allen said. The goal is long-term appreciation in value.

At a 10 unit town house at ... in which only three tenants bought their apartment upon conversion, Equity bought seven apartments for ... and syndicated five of them, he said. The apartments sold to investors for an average of $360,000, he said.

The nonbuying renters are continuing to live in the buildings at stabilized rents ranging from $320 to $450 a month. "They could have bought their apartment for about $70,000." Mr. Allen said, "but they say to themselves, "I've got a good deal—why should I pay $70,000 for my apartment?"

The purchasers of occupied apartments in the "aftermarket" include a number of professional converters themselves. Ivy Properties Ltd. based in White Plains, is a conversion sponsor that has also acquired occupied apartments from other sponsors for cash and resold them to individuals or groups of investors, generally at about a 25 percent discount from their value if vacant, said Steven Baruch, president.

The investor makes a 5 percent down payment and gets a 95 percent five-year note, on which he pays no interest for three years because under current tax laws accrued interest is deductible. After five years the note is convertible to a long-term self-liquidating loan. It is a nonrecourse loan-with no personal liability.

In Manhattan, Francis Greenburger, principal in Time Equities Inc., a large converter, said he made a bulk purchase of about 250 occupied apartments in four buildings for about $15 million in the last two months.

They have a retail, or vacancy, value of more than $30 million, he said. "The combined tax benefits in the holding period offset the carrying cost," he said.

Aaron Ziegelman, who in partnership with William K. Langfan has converted buildings with more than 5,000 apartments to cooperatives or condominiums, said he had sold at least 1,200 occupied apartments to outside investors. In condominiums all of his inventory is sold to a group such as a law firm or a corporation, since this form of investment ownership cannot have unfavorable tax effects on the building.

Occupied cooperatives are sold in packages of four apartments from four buildings, with no cash payment and 100 percent sponsor financing for 25 years, Mr. Ziegelman said. Apartments are priced at half of their vacancy value. Investors are in a 50 percent tax bracket.

The sponsor also does the selling for the investor-sometimes to a renter who decides belatedly to buy when inside discounts are no longer available. "The insider wants the old price and the investor wants the market price" Mr. Ziegelman said. "We get them together"

In the Citibank program, which is run through its mortgage center at the 399 Park Avenue branch, the buyer must make a $500 good-faith deposit to get pre-qualified for the specific amount he is eligible to borrow, From this comes a $150 appraisal fee and the rest is used to offset closing costs on the mortgage, a six-month adjustable-rate loan with five years of fixed payments and an initial rate of 11½ percent. It is usable in buildings in which Citibank has supplied primary financing,

When the apartment is vacated by the renter the bank adds to the debt 5 percent of the difference between the purchase price and the appraised value of the apartment when it becomes vacant. Copyright © (1984) by The New York Times Co. Reprinted with permission.

Joel F. Raven
Senior Vice President
And Managing Director

The CIT Group
Capital Investment, Inc.
270 Park Avenue
New York, NY 10017

March 12, 1990

Mr. Winston Allen, PhD
Creative Investor Services, Inc.
191 Post Road West
Westport, CT 06880
Dear Mr. Allen,

As a plaintiff you scored
A direct knockout punch,
So enjoy the attached,
Just make sure it's pre-lunch.

Best wishes for continued success and best regards.

Joel F. Raven/cs

Enclosure

    An *Ode to the Trials and Tribulations of Jury Duty*

    "Twas the day of the trial
    And near the courtroom,
    All the jurors were locked
    In their well furnished tomb,

    The pretrial motions
    Were argued and plead;
    The opening statements
    About to be read.

Judge Arber was ready
The lawyers in tow:
Young Collins, Sir Ostrow
And John Lankenau

Was 220's Board guilty?
Did Cross and Brown double cross?
Whosoever would win
Lots of dough could be lost.

The Allens, the Plaintiff
Were eager to start,
With Winston, the husband
Cast in the lead part.

The jury was shown in
And sworn in and seated,
The reporter was primed,
Justice poised to be meted

An opening statement
One more, then another,
It began, to appear
That this case was a mother.

And documents, documents
Documents more,
Quite soon there were documents
Table and floor.

A witness, a voire dire
Recross, redirect;
The lawyers were trying
To make punches connect.

The jurors awoke
To each new day with dread,
As visions of settlement
Danced in their heads.

Then all of a sudden,
Through windows ajar
There came such a ruckus
From a funeral car.

'Twas Glory Hallelujah!
With a faint Chinese spin
You could hear it in Beijing,
Shanghai or Guilin!

Our ears heard the Glory
Of the coming of the Lord,
To save us from Ostrow,
With whom we were bored.

And from out of the hallway
There arose such a clatter,
We jumped from our chairs
To see what was the matter.

When into the courtroom
Flew clerk Steve Tarasuk,
Who complained that some guard
Threw a punch, so he ducked..

The judge looked chagrined
And she motioned to Steve
That the jury was present
And he'd better just leave.

So we all sat there puzzled
Thinking "What was the cause?"
Fearing Steve would return
Swathed in bandage and gauze

Then an actress, more deps
And exhibits galore;
We began to surmise
That we could take no more.

Objection, exception
If your Honor pleases!
There's been no foundation;
That's legal misfeasance!

"Sustained! Overruled!
I'll allow that! BE SEATED!
The third time around,
That same question's unneeded!"

Exhibits by alphabet
Double and triple;
The judge said "OH VEY"
Laughter started to ripple.

And did young Shari Felix
Hear from Win in September?
Or June? Or July"?
Damn! She just can't remember.

And Ostrow, relentless,
His tongue fixed on wag;
He made us so ill
That we wanted to gag.

And then, 'cause good things and
As suns set in the west,
The Plaintiff and versus
Decided to rest.

The jury rejoiced,
No more weeks need be scuttled,
"Till young Collins announced
That he had a rebuttal.

And so back to the courtroom
For a new day we went
As we realized with fear
One more week could be spent.

The finally arguments,
Closing, we learned;
Did the Allens just screw up?
Or did they get burned?

The judge gave instructions
On just how we should think,
And how relevant law
With the facts should be linked.

We looked at exhibits
And argued for hours,
And couldn't agree
On intent or our powers,

Instructions reread
Testimony reheard,
We listened intently
To each spoken word.

And then lo and behold!
Don't believe that I heard it!
Wed took one more vote
And we got us a verdict!

A quick note to the judge,
One more trek down the hall,
The clerk asked the foreman
If we had made our call.

The courtroom was hushed
Suspense too hard to bear
For the Allens it seemed
St. Nick soon would be there.

Now a word for the next
Who get called for a jury
Just take it in stride
There is no use for fury.

Don't bribe to escape it
Don't be so forlorn
For Hell hath a jury
For duty suborned.

United States Patent

Allen

Patent Number: 5,685,829

Date of Patent: Nov. 11, 1997

HAND OPERATED HYDRO-THERAPY DEVICE

Inventor: Winston E. Allen,
          Westport, Conn. 06880

Appl. No.: 395,899
Filed: Feb. 28, 1995

Primary Examiner—Danton D. DeMille
Attorney, Agent, or Firm—James J. McKeever

Related U. S. Application Data

Continuation-in part of Ser.... June 21, 1992

ABSTRACT

A hydro-therapy device for use with home or club showers and physical therapist which consists of a flexible hose to connect to a diverter valve that is in turn connected to a water source. A shower head of choice is also connected to the diverter valve so that the user may select a regular shower or a hydro-therapy treatment to a selected portion of his body. The control nozzle of the present invention is connected to the other end of the flexible hose. The control nozzle is what created the hydro-therapy high pressure single stream of water. The user simply places the diverter valve in the hydro-therapy position, points the control valve at that part of the body that he wishes to treat and slide the on/off switch to the on position and the treatment begins.

1 Claim, 5 Drawing Sheets

What is claimed is:

1. A portable device for performing personal hydro-therapy with a single stream of pressurized water comprising:

an elongated hollow housing, said housing having an entrance end and exit end for the water, said housing further effective in passing a flow of pressurized water therethrough, said entrance end connected through a plurality of plumbing pipe connections to a flexible conduit means; said flexible conduit means connected to a diverter valve; said diverter valve provided with an alternative diverter capable of selectively directing pressurized water to a shower head or said flexible conduit means, said diverter valve connected to a pressurized water source;

said elongated hollow housing is provided with a thumb switch, located on the outside wall surface of said elongated hollow housing, said thumb switch connected through a longitudinal opening in said housing to a piston in a centrally positioned piston housing inside said elongated hollow housing, said piston housing having a circular cross section supported in a spaced central location allowing the free flow of water all around the outside of the piston housing, said housing hollow housing exit end having an opening shaped to concentrate water exiting the housing into a single stream of pressurized water, said piston having an exit end which includes a portion which enters the hollow housing exit end opening for controlling the single stream of pressurized water, said piston having an O-ring on said exit end for sealing with the opening in the hollow housing exit in said piston having two additional O rings for sealing the central portion of the piston housing from water, said piston in said piston housing is connected to said thumb switch that is adapted to being placed in an off position, a fully on position or anywhere in between by the movement of said thumb switch,

said portion of the exit end of the piston moves within the hollow housing exit end opening to control the size and force of the pressured water flow out the exit end of the hollow housing thereby producing a pressurized single stream of hydro-therapeutic water in a force of from about 40 to about 85 ppi to whatever location on the body of the user that may be desired.

Xerox World
October 1978

After 40 years ... Xerography in Retrospect: Carlson, Haloid Xerox & the 914

Both of these men made fortunes in xerography. Their backgrounds and personalities were very different, yet both were reflective men who were concerned with more than money and business. They saw challenges, not problems. They accepted setbacks as temporary. They lived up to their performances because they expected it of themselves. They were rich in the fullest sense of the word.

Chester Carlson helped Joe Wilson realize his dream. Carlson, the inventor of xerography, filed his first patent in 1937. His first successful image was made in 1938. Over the next nine years, he tried to sell his ideas to more than twenty companies, including RCA, Remington Rand, General Electric, Kodak, and IBM. They all turned him down, wondering why someone would need a machine to do something you could do with carbon paper. Although Carlson was often frustrated by the lack of interest in his invention, he never quit. Finally, he hooked up with Wilson, and both made fortunes with xerography. Carlson earned more than $200 million and Wilson $100 million because they could not be discouraged. Their careers exemplify some of the principles in this book.

Carlson was never on the regular Xerox payroll, though Wilson, CEO, made several offers. Instead, Carlson preferred the independence of working as a consultant. He died in 1968 of a heart attack at the age of sixty-two. A day before his death his wife asked him if he had any unfulfilled desires. "Just one," he said. "I would like to die a poor man." When he died, he had given away more than $150 million. Carlson was truly an inspiration for this book. He had a vision, he set high goals, he recognized a need, and seized opportunities. He took risks and he climbed aboard the fast track. And he was a philanthropist.

Wilson was a graduate of the Harvard Business School. His father was president of Haloid before him, and his grandfather had served as mayor of Rochester. Unlike Carlson, Wilson did not come from a humble background. But they were similar in that they both thought like successful business owners and knew how to resolve difficult problems. Wilson was an outgoing person and a student of literature. His speeches were as likely to contain quotes from Byron and Dostoyevsky as they were to contain the latest earnings and revenue numbers. Even after the company became successful he would often lunch at his desk so that he could catch up on his reading. He welcomed involvement in community affairs, often speaking about the obligations of successful enterprises to contribute to society.

On September 16, 1959, twenty-one years after Carlson made his famous first image, the Xerox 914 was announced. *Fortune* Magazine would later call it the most successful product ever marketed in America.

One thing we learn from these two men is that the desire for money is not a strong enough reason to go into business. The most important thing you learn from their experiences is that they loved what they did. Secondly, they showed that you need to choose something that you are gifted at. Wilson never liked it when people referred to Xerox during its growth years as a Cinderella story. The company *earned* its success, he said. The only magic was the magic of hard work. Copyright © (1978) Xerox World. Reprinted with permission.

Xerox World

The Founding of the Xerox Corporation

The Xerox Corporation that we know today began as the Haloid Company back in 1949 when the company had just bought the license to use the xerographic process for image duplication. This process was devised by Chester Carlson and researchers at the Battelle Memorial Institute and introduced to the American Optical Society in 1948. An internal company publication reported that the Haloid Company after World War II was headed for trouble.

While revenues of the small Rochester, N.Y. firm were increasing, its earnings were shrinking, and the prognosis for improvements was poor. Since its founding in 1906, Haloid had grown in a modest but consistent fashion by making and selling photographic paper and photocopying equipment, even during the Depression years. But the booming war years produced a number of tough competitors with improved products. The Haloid market share began to shrink, and worse, there was nothing in the works for the future.

Joseph C. Wilson, who was about to assume Haloid's leadership from his retiring father, decided that the answer lay in acquiring a promising new technology. As fate would have it, there was at that time a new idea looking for a company. The two were introduced in the July 1944 issue of *Radio News*, a technical periodical brought to the attention of Dr. John H. Dissuader, Haloid's research head. In the magazine was an article on electrophotography. Dissuader showed it to Wilson, and they agreed this process warranted a closer look.

Battle Memorial Institute, a non-profit research organization in Columbus, Ohio, had recently acquired the rights from an unknown inventor named Chester Carlson, who had tried in vain to interest large companies in his process.

While working as a patent attorney for an electronics firm in New York, Carlson had some business dealings with Battle physicist Russell Dayton. As they were chatting, he handed Dayton one of his patents and asked if Bastille might be interested. It was. Carlson demonstrated his process in

Columbus, and when he finished, Dayton told his colleagues, "However crude this may seem, this is the first time any of you have seen a reproduction made without any chemical reaction and by a dry process."

A deal was struck, with Battle agreeing to do the development work for 60 percent of any royalties, though they were still unsure of just what good use would come of this new process. Their development work was crucial: In selenium, Battle researchers found the ideal reusable photoconductor. One of the Earth's 105 known chemical elements, selenium proved to be much more effective than the sulfur Carlson had been using. Battle also devised the developer—a mixture of dry ink particles (toner) and "carrier" beads that remains the basic formula today.

... A contract was signed, effective January 1, 1947, which essentially gave Haloid a license to develop a xerographic machine. *Xerox World* reported that Wilson later wondered aloud why Battle gambled on tiny Haloid. "Financially, we were very limited," Wilson said. "We had a limited marketing organization and a limited research group. I guess what sold them was that we were going to make or break it."

The parties also agreed that electrophotography, the word Carlson coined, was too cumbersome. An Ohio State classics professor came up with the name *xerography* from the Greek words for "dry" and "writing." Through subsequent contracts with Battle, Haloid acquired more and more of the development burden. Marshalling its meager resources, it introduced its first xerographic machine—the Xerox (with a capital "X") Copier—in 1950. It was slow, dirty, and required a number of carefully executed manual operations to produce a decent copy. But fortunately, they had stumbled into a ready-made market. Slow as it was as a document copier, the Xerox Copier proved to be a quick master-maker for a new type of small office printing press requiring paper masters which ordinarily had to be typed by hand.

In 1955 came Copilot, the first automated xerographic machine. It produced enlarged prints on a continuous roll from microfilm originals and spawned a line of Xerox Microsystems products that are still turning significant pro. Copilot was also the first product to use a rotating drum, instead of a plate as the photoconductive surface—an ingenious solution to the problems of how to make copies quickly.

By 1955, Haloid sales were $21 million, three times those of 1947. Fueled with revenue and confidence, Haloid changed its name to Haloid Xerox and prepared to develop what its market research showed that people wanted—a fast, cheap, convenient office copier. But was xerography the method, and Haloid the means?

Though the company was doing well, Wilson feared that revenues were simply not enough to stage the development of a xerographic office copier, and even considered offering to share the prospect with larger companies that had the wherewithal. But just as Carlson was turned away, so were Wilson's probes met with disinterest. Haloid, forced to either quit or go for broke, took the latter course, staking all it had, and a lot it didn't have, on a product no one could say would either work or staff.

In the fall of 1959, the world saw the 914 copier (so named because it could copy on sheets as large as 9 by 14 inches). By the end of 1962, ten thousand had been shipped—many more than had been predicted—and the manufacturers were backlogged with orders. And optimistic predictions that are typical of 914 would do ten thousand copies a month was also proved much too low. In short, the 914 was an astounding success, one of the most successful single products ever made. It launched a giant corporation and revolutionized an industry.

In 1961, Haloid Xerox took the name of Xerox, and its stock was listed on the New York Stock Exchange. XRX was a hot issue even in those go years. Straining the phenomenon it had created, Xerox frantically tried to keep up with the demand for its products, while hiring employees rapidly, building a manufacturing and research complex in Webster, and recruiting an entire sales and service force.

It was an enormous gamble that paid off in spades. Some $40 million had been spent to develop the 914. The feat was accomplished by pouring profits back into research, by heavy borrowing, and by convincing investors to accept more shares instead of dividends. But mostly it was done on inspiration and courage. Like few others in their time, the Haloid people were believers. Their motivation created one of the most spectacular business success stories of the century.

About the Author

Winston E. Allen, PhD, is a New York and Connecticut real estate developer and securities dealer. In 1962, he founded his broker-dealership. He has been a Fulbright scholar and a Fordham University professor. He restructured Xerox Corporation's international training facility, and he taught graduate business school at American and George Washington universities. He and his wife, Ruby, have resided in Westport, Connecticut, since 1975. A son, Vaughn, is an educator, and a daughter, Julie, is an engineer.

Index

Note: Page entries followed by "*p*" indicate that the reference is to a picture.

978-0-595-68258-4
0-595-68258-8

Printed in the United States
202580BV00003B/130-192/P